MEASURING A *changing* NATION

Modern Methods for the 2000 Census

Michael L. Cohen, Andrew A. White, and
Keith F. Rust, *Editors*

Panel on Alternative Census Methodologies

Committee on National Statistics

Commission on Behavioral and Social Sciences
and Education

National Research Council

NATIONAL ACADEMY PRESS
Washington, D.C. 1999

NOTICE: The project that is the subject of this report was approved by the Governing Board of the National Research Council, whose members are drawn from the councils of the National Academy of Sciences, the National Academy of Engineering, and the Institute of Medicine. The members of the committee responsible for the report were chosen for their special competences and with regard for appropriate balance.

The National Academy of Sciences is a private, nonprofit, self-perpetuating society of distinguished scholars engaged in scientific and engineering research, dedicated to the furtherance of science and technology and to their use for the general welfare. Upon the authority of the charter granted to it by the Congress in 1863, the Academy has a mandate that requires it to advise the federal government on scientific and technical matters. Dr. Bruce Alberts is president of the National Academy of Sciences.

The National Academy of Engineering was established in 1964, under the charter of the National Academy of Sciences, as a parallel organization of outstanding engineers. It is autonomous in its administration and in the selection of its members, sharing with the National Academy of Sciences the responsibility for advising the federal government. The National Academy of Engineering also sponsors engineering programs aimed at meeting national needs, encourages education and research, and recognizes the superior achievements of engineers. Dr. William A. Wulf is president of the National Academy of Engineering.

The Institute of Medicine was established in 1970 by the National Academy of Sciences to secure the services of eminent members of appropriate professions in the examination of policy matters pertaining to the health of the public. The Institute acts under the responsibility given to the National Academy of Sciences by its congressional charter to be an adviser to the federal government and, upon its own initiative, to identify issues of medical care, research, and education. Dr. Kenneth I. Shine is president of the Institute of Medicine.

The National Research Council was organized by the National Academy of Sciences in 1916 to associate the broad community of science and technology with the Academy's purposes of furthering knowledge and advising the federal government. Functioning in accordance with general policies determined by the Academy, the Council has become the principal operating agency of both the National Academy of Sciences and the National Academy of Engineering in providing services to the government, the public, and the scientific and engineering communities. The Council is administered jointly by both Academies and the Institute of Medicine. Dr. Bruce Alberts and Dr. William A. Wulf are chairman and vice-chairman, respectively, of the National Research Council.

This project is supported by funds provided by the Bureau of the Census, U.S. Department of Commerce, under contract number 50-YABC-5-66005. Support of the work of the Committee on National Statistics is provided by a consortium of federal agencies through a grant from the National Science Foundation (Number SBR-9709489). Any opinions, findings, conclusions, or recommendations expressed in this publication are those of the author(s) and do not necessarily reflect the views of the organizations or agencies that provided support for this project.

International Standard Book Number 0-309-06444-9

Additional copies of this report are available from National Academy Press, 2101 Constitution Avenue, N.W., Box 285, Washington, D.C. 20055. Call (800) 624-6242 or (202) 334-3313 (in the Washington metropolitan area). This report is also available online at http://www.nap.edu

Printed in the United States of America

PANEL ON ALTERNATIVE CENSUS METHODOLOGIES

iii

Acknowledgments

The Panel on Alternative Census Methodologies thanks the many people who contributed to the preparation of this, the panel's final report.

We thank, first, the staff of our sponsor, the Bureau of the Census, who provided detailed and informative presentations on the wide variety of aspects of decennial census processes relevant to the panel's charge. We are especially indebted to Ruth Ann Killion, who was always available to panel members and staff to answer the large number of technical questions that came up, who worked hard to make materials available to the panel as soon as possible, and who provided the panel with superb presentations on a variety of issues. We also thank the many other staff who played a role in the preparation or presentation of material to the panel: Florence Abramson, William Bell, Deborah Bolton, Geraldine Burt, Jon Clark, Cynthia Z.F. Clark, Mary Davis, Howard Dennis, James Farber, Robert Fay, Linda Franz, Edison Gore, Richard Griffin, Joan Hill, Howard Hogan, David Hubble, Cary Isaki, Jay Keller, Edward Kobilarcik, Donna Kostanich, Charlene Leggieri, Robert Marx, Carol Miller, William Mockovak, Joel Morrison, Mary Mulry, Alfredo Navarro, Arona Pistiner, Ronald Prevost, David Raglin, Marvin Raines, Magda Ramos, Martha Riche, Harry Scarr, Eric Schindler, Paula Schneider, Rajendra Singh, Dennis Stoudt, John Thompson, Elizabeth Ann Vacca, Frank Vitrano, Preston J. Waite, Judith Waldrop, Kirsten West, David Whitford, Henry Woltman, and Tommy Wright.

The panel also is indebted to several experts who were invited to contribute to the public discussions: Wayne Fuller, Iowa State University; Benjamin King, National Opinion Research Center (retired); Janet

Norwood, Urban Institute; and Nora Cate Schaeffer, University of Wisconsin.

The panel was guided and assisted by very capable and dedicated staff of the Committee on National Statistics (CNSTAT). Andrew White directed the study initially, and he remained very active in the panel's activities after Michael Cohen took over as study director during the final stage of the panel. Both worked skillfully and tirelessly at coordinating panel activities, interacting with Census Bureau staff and others, and guiding and assisting in the preparation of our reports. Miron Straf, CNSTAT director, took great interest in the panel's activities from the outset and provided us with much insight and guidance. Constance Citro also gave us the great benefit of her considerable experience with census issues, as did CNSTAT consultant Meyer Zitter, who attended all of the panel's meetings and was a great source of wisdom on census processes. Agnes Gaskin was enormously helpful in making all of the detailed arrangements concerning the meetings, distribution of panel materials, and myriad details. In addition, she assisted greatly in preparing the draft manuscripts of the interim and final reports, and she was always someone that could be relied on to boost staff morale. Finally, Jamie Casey was excellent at summarizing meetings in notes that the panel found extremely useful.

Eugenia Grohman, associate director for reports of the Commission on Behavioral and Social Sciences and Education, enormously improved the report through her superlative technical editing. The presentation of the report is substantially improved due to her expertise and hard work. In addition, Genie ably shepherded the panel through report review and report production.

This report has been reviewed in draft form by individuals chosen for their diverse perspectives and technical expertise, in accordance with procedures approved by the NRC's Report Review Committee. The purpose of this independent review is to provide candid and critical comments that will assist the institution in making the published report as sound as possible and to ensure that the report meets institutional standards for objectivity, evidence, and responsiveness to the study charge. The review comments and draft manuscript remain confidential to protect the integrity of the deliberative process. We thank the following individuals for their participation in the review of this report: Barbara Bailar, National Opinion Research Center, Chicago, Ill.; Norman Bradburn, Vice President for Research, University of Chicago; Lawrence Brown, Department of Statistics, University of Pennsylvania; Eugene Ericksen, Department of Statistics, Temple University; Stephen Fienberg, Department of Statistics, Carnegie Mellon University; Louis Gordon, Palo Alto, Calif.; Stephen Heeringa, Institute for Social Research, University of Michigan; Roderick

J.A. Little, School of Public Health, University of Michigan; James Morgan, Institute for Social Research, University of Michigan (emeritus); and Samuel Preston, Dean of Arts and Sciences, University of Pennsylvania. While the individuals listed above have provided constructive comments and suggestions, it must be emphasized that responsibility for the final content of this report rests entirely with the authoring panel and the institution.

Finally, I have the pleasure of thanking my fellow panel colleagues. Over the 3 years of the panel's duration, they have remained committed and enthusiastic in ensuring that the panel met its charge to the full. Panel members were willing to devote considerable time between meetings to deliberating over issues for which they had special expertise, to reviewing the information that we were provided, and in drafting and reviewing material for our reports. It has been a pleasure working with them and to have enjoyed their support throughout.

Keith Rust, *Chair*
Panel on Alternative Census Methodologies

Contents

Preface

In April 1995 the Bureau of the Census of the U.S. Department of Commerce asked the National Research Council's Committee on National Statistics to form a study panel to review plans and research and make recommendations regarding the design of the 2000 census. The Panel on Alternative Census Methodologies was set up to carry out the study, building on the work of the predecessor Committee on National Statistics Panel to Evaluate Alternative Census Methods.

The charge to our panel was to review the Census Bureau's plans for the 2000 census and to make recommendations regarding the census design. Specifically, we were asked to review results of the 1995 and 1996 census tests, particularly with respect to the sample design for nonresponse follow-up and the planned integrated coverage measurement sample design and estimation procedures for the 2000 census, to recommend additional field tests and research to carry out in the near term and in the 2000 census, and, finally, to review the use of administrative records in the 2000 census. In response to our charge, we have issued two interim reports (National Research Council, 1996, 1997b) and a letter report (National Research Council, 1997a). We last met in June 1998, preparatory to drafting this, our final report.

Our report was in the final stages of report review, editing, and production when the U.S. Supreme Court issued a decision on January 25, 1999, which finds that, according to federal law (Title 13 of the U.S. Code), sampling may not be used to obtain census counts for purposes of congressional apportionment. The report contains language (Chapter 2, pages 34-35) that anticipated the possibility that the court would reach the

conclusion it did. Barring a change to Title 13, the panel's recommendations pertaining to sampling for the purpose of apportionment are moot
for the 2000 census. The only changes that have been made in the report
as a result of the decision are the addition of portions of this preface and
three footnotes that refer the reader to the preface.

Decisions about the best methodology for such an important and
complex operation as the decennial census require extensive research and
careful deliberation. All of the members of our panel are grateful to have
had the opportunity to consider methodological issues for the census in
the year 2000 and beyond.

Keith Rust, *Chair*
Panel on Alternative Census Methodologies

MEASURING A *changing* NATION

Executive Summary

This final report of the Panel on Alternative Census Methodologies provides an assessment of the Census Bureau's plans for the 2000 census as of the time of the 1998 census dress rehearsal. It examines changes in census plans following, and to a modest extent in reaction to, the panel's second interim report, regarding the use of sampling for nonresponse follow-up, construction of the master address file, use of multiple response modes and respondent-friendly questionnaires, and the use of administrative records. It also describes evaluation plans for the census dress rehearsal and plans for data collection and experimentation during the 2000 census. Most of the results from the dress rehearsal were not yet available to the panel, so this report does not offer any suggested changes to 2000 census plans in response to the dress rehearsal.

The Census Bureau plans to introduce several new features for the 2000 census: enhanced procedures for developing the master address list to which census forms are mailed; modern mail survey techniques to enhance response, including revised forms and multiple mail contacts; making census forms available in a variety of public places; use of random sampling during nonresponse follow-up; an expanded coverage measurement survey of 750,000 housing units to obtain information about census coverage rates; and incorporation of the results of the nonresponse follow-up and the coverage measurement survey into the census counts using statistical estimation procedures.[1]

---

[1]The U.S. Supreme Court ruled on January 25, 1999, that sampling cannot be used to collect census counts for purposes of congressional apportionment; see Preface.

NEW CENSUS PLANS

Address List and Mail Procedures

Of all the new census procedures, producing a nearly complete address list and obtaining a high mail response rate remain the cornerstone of a high-quality census. The other procedures are designed to complement these two main steps by ensuring that high quality is maintained even if address list development and the mail return process fall short of perfection.

During the 1990s the Census Bureau conducted an address list improvement program that included making use of U.S. Postal Service files and input from local officials. Because these efforts were not sufficient, the Bureau has instituted plans for a nationwide field check of addresses prior to the 2000 census. The panel strongly endorses these newly instituted procedures.

Through research early in the 1990s, the Census Bureau also determined that provision of a replacement form targeted to mail nonrespondents would likely yield substantial improvements in mail response rates. The panel endorsed both the process used to evaluate that research and the subsequent changes to the form and to the techniques used to encourage mail response. However, all research regarding the mailing of a replacement form was specific only for households that failed to respond to the initial mailing—and the Census Bureau subsequently determined that it could not implement such a targeted replacement operation in the time available. Therefore, the 1998 census dress rehearsal tested the process of sending a replacement form to all households. The panel believes that it is critical to measure the effects of the use of an untargeted replacement form, especially its effects on respondent cooperation and the effectiveness of the unduplication process used for households that return both forms. An analysis of dress rehearsal results should be performed to help decide whether to use an untargeted replacement form in the 2000 census.

Making forms available at public places was successfully tested in 1995. If the dress rehearsal results confirm that this program is beneficial (i.e., if the number of duplicate submissions of census questionnaires is considered small or if the unduplication process is considered to be of high enough quality), the panel believes this procedure will afford some gains in response at relatively little cost. In addition, the concept may have public relations benefits, as suggested in work with focus groups.

Sampling for Nonresponse Follow-Up

The panel has concluded that a properly designed and well-executed sampling plan for field follow-up of census mail nonrespondents will save over $100 million (assuming an overall sampling rate of 75 percent). Furthermore, sampling for nonresponse follow-up will reduce the Census Bureau's total workload, which will permit improvements in the control and management of field operations, and will allow more complete follow-up of difficult cases that could lead to an increase in the quality of the census data collected by enumerators. In addition, nonresponse follow-up interviews could be completed in a more timely fashion, which would lead to improvements in quality when the planned integrated coverage measurement operation is used.

Of course, sampling for nonresponse follow-up will add sampling variability to census counts. However, imprecision in the census counts at low levels of geographic aggregation due to added variance through use of sampling for nonresponse follow-up will not cause any systematic biases, because under sampling for nonresponse follow-up only characteristics of people found in a tract contribute to the estimates for that tract. Furthermore, the relative amount of variance due to sampling decreases as the population of an area increases, and the amount of sampling variance can be measured statistically. As a result of this, and also due to the possibly higher quality of collected data resulting from the use of sampling, the panel believes that sampling for nonresponse follow-up will provide data of equal or better quality when used for congressional apportionment and that it will approximately replicate, at lower levels of aggregation, what would be obtained with 100 percent follow-up.

The panel further concludes that the prespecified nature of the sampling design for nonresponse follow-up and the fact that enumerators will not know whether households they are *not* visiting are mail respondents or nonrespondents that are not sampled ensures that sampling does not present a new opportunity for manipulation of census counts by enumerators.

Adjusting for Differential Undercoverage

Because the master address list is incomplete, because households are sometimes missed in listed housing units, and because individuals who live in otherwise enumerated households are at times missed, there is (gross) undercoverage in the decennial census. At the same time, people can be enumerated in multiple ways, possibly at several residences, so there is also (gross) overcoverage in the decennial census. The difference between undercoverage and overcoverage is referred to as net undercoverage, and this is what is relevant to the allocation of political representation and public funds. This net undercoverage affects some groups more than others—that is, the census has *differential* (net) undercoverage—and there are demographic groups for which this differential undercoverage has persisted over several censuses.

The 1950 through 1990 decennial censuses all made use of various evaluation programs to assess the extent of gross and net census undercoverage and its causes. The only cost-effective methodology available for measuring the degree of differential undercoverage for subnational areas is a large-scale post-enumeration survey coupled with dual-system estimation.

Dual-system estimation, the methodology used in 1990 to join the information from the post-enumeration survey and the census to measure net census undercoverage, depends on several assumptions. After considering the criticisms related to the validity of, and the impact of departures from these assumptions, which have been used to argue against the use of integrated coverage measurement to produce official population counts, the panel concludes that the criticisms of this approach are not compelling reasons to halt plans to use integrated coverage measurement in 2000. If the Supreme Court prohibits use of integrated coverage measurement for apportionment, the panel still strongly supports a post-enumeration survey of the currently budgeted size of 750,000, for purposes other than apportionment.

Estimation Methods

The decennial census, as planned for 2000, will require estimation methods that were not needed or used in 1990. They include supplying imputed records as a result of sampling for nonresponse follow-up and for carrying the results of the dual-system estimation down to small areas. The Census Bureau has made an effort to keep these estimation methods as simple as possible. While the panel supports this decision for the 2000 census, it hopes that several more promising techniques can be adequately tested over the next decade and used in 2010 if shown to have advantages over the techniques used in 2000.

EXPERIMENTATION IN THE 2000 CENSUS

As the U.S. population continues to change in various ways, the best methods for enumerating the population also change. Therefore, a cycle of experimentation and data collection during a census followed by evaluation, further development, and experimentation and testing between censuses, is necessary for an effective census methodology. The decennial census provides a unique opportunity for testing new methodologies because of its size and its general level of public acceptance and awareness. Data collection is essential to support later simulation studies and generally to understand what happened. Plans for research experimentation and data collection during the 2000 census are now being finalized. These plans begin the process of developing methodologies for 2010.

One concern with respect to testing as part of the decennial census is whether it is possible to predict 11 or 12 years in advance what methodologies might be effective. After all, technologies change at a rapid pace and the U.S. population itself is dynamic. Yet in previous censuses the Census Bureau staff carried out tests that were useful for advancing census methodology for the subsequent census. An important example is the introduction of a mailout/mailback census, which was tested in 1960 and introduced on a broad scale in 1970.

When unanticipated problems arise during the decennial census that require additional funds, field staff, or other resources, there is a natural tendency to draw off resources from research experimentation and data collection. Unfortunately, this may "mortgage the future" of census taking for smaller, immediate benefits. Many issues involving the methodology to be used for the 2000 census would have been clarified if additional data collection had been incorporated into the 1990 census.

The panel strongly supports a renewal and modest expansion of the suggestion by a previous National Research Council panel for a master trace sample—that is, a sample of tracts in which essential information on all respondents with respect to enumeration is saved. Given the variety of innovations in the 2000 census, it would be extremely useful if the planned data management system could collect and save for research purposes a trace sample in, say, 100 tracts spread around the country. The trace sample would provide information about phases of data collection, which would be extremely valuable in guiding future methodological advances.

Planning for a decennial census begins at least 10 years before the first questionnaire is mailed. Some decisions must be made relatively early in the decade because of the need to procure equipment or because of limited testing opportunities. While the panel supports the fundamental decisions that the Census Bureau has made in planning for the 2000 census regarding sampling for nonresponse follow-up and integrated coverage measurement, various decisions that the Census Bureau was required to make early in the 1990s that cannot be changed until the 2010 census planning cycle—some supported by this panel, some not—need to be revisited for 2010. Two examples are whether the Census Bureau should in sampling for nonresponse follow-up—in combination with mail response—be obligated to directly enumerate at least 90 percent of the households in each tract, and whether it would be more effective for the Census Bureau to make use of estimation methods that borrow information across states.

TIME FOR PLANNING

All of the innovations planned for first use in the 2000 census, along with the methods used in 1990, have received their final test in the 1998 census dress rehearsal in Sacramento, California; Columbia, South Carolina, and its 11 surrounding counties; and Menominee County, Wisconsin. The evaluation studies based on the dress rehearsal will provide the final, important input to the decisions the Census Bureau must make as to the final plans for the 2000 census. The 37 evaluation studies are well designed, covering all aspects of census taking. The panel considers it important that they be completed in time to inform the decisions for 2000.

Finally, there is clearly a need for the Census Bureau to have sufficient time to plan whether the 2000 census may or may not use statistical sampling in either or both nonresponse follow-up and integrated coverage measurement. The fact that the Bureau is now less than 15 months from the start of the 2000 census without a firm decision on that issue presents an enormous problem to the Bureau in planning and implementing the complex process that is the U.S. decennial census.

1

Introduction

The decennial census is used to determine political apportionment, redistricting, and fund allocation for a wide variety of federal, state, and local programs. Many of these uses are mandated by laws, which impose various constraints, including deadlines, and limitations on the information that can be collected and on the statistical methods that can be used. Participation in the census is mandatory, but as a practical matter it is not enforced. Consequently, there is less than full participation in the census, and various means are used to compensate for the missing data, which are vital given the uses of census data.

In April 1995 the Bureau of the Census of the U.S. Department of Commerce asked the Committee on National Statistics of the National Research Council (NRC) to form a study panel to review plans and research for and make recommendations regarding the design of the 2000 census. The current panel was formed to further consider many of the issues raised by the earlier Panel to Evaluate Alternative Census Methods (National Research Council, 1994). It was charged with reviewing results of the 1995 and 1996 census tests, particularly with respect to sample design for nonresponse follow-up and the planned integrated coverage measurement sample design and estimation procedures for the 2000 census; recommending additional field tests and research to carry out in the near term and in the 2000 census; and reviewing the use of administrative records in the 2000 census.

As required, the panel has issued two interim reports (National Research Council 1996, 1997b). The first report focused on the use of statistical procedures, especially sampling, in the 2000 census. The second report provided refinements in several areas, including plans and research in the use of sampling for nonresponse follow-up, plans for constructing the master address file, plans and testing of multiple response modes and the use of respondent-friendly questionnaires, and plans for the use of administrative records. The panel also issued a letter report on the problems raised by the use of an untargeted replacement questionnaire (National Research Council, 1997a).

The rest of this chapter provides an overview of census innovations and a description of the 1998 census dress rehearsal and the associated evaluation studies. Chapter 2 reviews key findings of the panel with regard to the six main processes (outlined below) that the Census Bureau plans to implement for the first time in the 2000 census. Chapter 3 reviews in more detail a number of Census Bureau decisions concerning how these activities are to be carried out in 2000 and what might be done differently in the 2010 census. Chapter 4 presents a discussion of three important technical criticisms in the statistical literature against use of integrated coverage measurement. Finally, Chapter 5 comments on current Census Bureau plans for research and experimentation and data collection during the 2000 census, looking forward to the 2010 census. A glossary of census terminology is also provided.

INNOVATIONS IN CENSUS METHODOLOGY

The basic approach to the 2000 census that the Census Bureau proposed in 1996 is either a direct continuation or else closely related to the methods that have been used since 1960:

- The Census Bureau develops a comprehensive list of residential dwellings in the United States.
- A census form is mailed to each of those housing units.
- Households are asked to return the completed forms by mail.
- Households that do not return the forms are visited by enumerators.

The major problems in quality and cost that arise in the census result from the fact that these four procedures do not work perfectly by themselves and they do not interact perfectly. First, some households are missing from the address list used for mailing forms. In some cases, the Postal Service fails to deliver the form to the household, often because the address is inadequate or the Postal Service erroneously considers the dwelling to be vacant. Second, it is expected that more than 30 percent of American housing units in 2000 will not return the form delivered to them. Third, for a portion of those that are returned, there will be persons missed and other errors of fact. Finally, enumerators often fail either to contact household members or to convince them to respond, even after numerous and expensive field follow-up visits.

The Census Bureau has developed a number of revised procedures to update and improve each component of this fundamental structure. (See the glossary of census terms for details regarding language that appears below.) These are procedures that the Census Bureau now plans to implement for the first time in the 2000 census (although some are contingent on decisions by Congress and the courts):

• The Census Bureau has made and is making use of enhanced procedures for developing the address list to which the census forms are mailed. These procedures have involved efforts to build the address list throughout the decade (instead of relying solely on a rush effort as the census approaches, using sources of variable quality) and included the use of the previous decennial census mailing list.

• Each household will be sent a letter notifying it that a census form will be mailed shortly, followed by the arrival of the census form, followed by a reminder to complete the form. As this report is being completed, it is unclear whether the Census Bureau will make use of the mailing of a second census form to every housing unit (not only the nonresponding ones, as was once proposed but is now considered to be operationally infeasible).

• Census forms will be made available in a variety of public places that have previously not been used for this purpose. Households that believe they did not receive a form or individuals who believe they were not included on any household form may complete a form and return it to the Census Bureau. In addition, people may call the Census Bureau to provide their responses.

• Households that fail to return the mailed census form by a specific date will be followed up on a sample basis. A random sample of these households (including those that were classified as vacant by the Postal Service) will be contacted to obtain the requested data. This approach represents a major departure from past census practice, in which follow-up was attempted for *all* nonrespondent households.[1] The Census Bureau believes that this plan will be advantageous for three reasons: (1) to ensure that nonresponse follow-up is finished within a reasonable time; (2) to control the costs of nonresponse follow-up (the primary cause of

---

[1]Sampling for long-form information, however, has been used in the decennial census since 1940.

census cost overruns); and (3) to improve census quality, especially when used in conjunction with plans for integrated coverage measurement, by expediting field operations. The proportion of nonresponding households included in the follow-up sample will vary by geographic area (census tract). The proportion to be sampled will be determined by the proportion of households in a census tract that return the census forms by mail. The higher the proportion that do so, the smaller will be the proportion of nonrespondents who are visited by enumerators—but at least one-third of mail nonrespondents will be included in the sample from each tract, regardless of the mail return rate.

• There will be an additional survey of 750,000 housing units conducted after the nonresponse follow-up is concluded. This post-enumeration survey, much larger than that conducted in previous censuses, is designed to obtain information about housing units that were missed by the initial census process and about individuals who were omitted from or erroneously included on their household census form (and households included in the wrong geographic area).[2] The post-enumeration survey is an effort at data collection that is independent, operationally, of the census—that is, it does not rely on other aspects of census processes. This approach assists in supporting the statistical assumption of the independence of the two enumeration processes used in estimation associated with the post-enumeration survey. By reconciling the results of this independent survey with inputs from previous stages of the census, information is obtained about the number and characteristics of people who were missed (or erroneously included) in the initial or standard census process. The integrated coverage measurement survey is very similar to the post-enumeration survey conducted in 1990, but with two important differences: it is planned to be nearly five times as large, and the results are planned to be incorporated into the single set of official census figures rather than presented separately as an adjustment. This survey along with the resulting estimation, is referred to as integrated coverage measurement.

• The results of the nonresponse follow-up and the integrated coverage measurement will be incorporated into the official census counts using statistical estimation and imputation procedures. Accordingly, the

---

[2]A very important problem that results in both census omissions and erroneous enumerations in otherwise enumerated households is that for a certain portion of the population there is ambiguity of residence and household composition. This ambiguity includes the following situations: people with several residences, people living temporarily at an address, people whose usual residence is not where they sleep, children living with other relatives during the week or children in joint custody arrangements, and people with commuter marriages.

census figures released on December 31, 2000, for states and on April 1, 2001,[3] for blocks for use in congressional redistricting and other purposes will reflect the results of these data collection procedures, accounting for the sampling used in nonresponse follow-up and integrated coverage measurement.

Each of these steps plays a role in improving the quality of the census. Developing a high-quality address list (geographically referenced to the correct location on the census block boundary maps) and obtaining a high mail return rate are crucial to an accurate census. Both reduce reliance on the use of nonresponse follow-up and on integrated coverage measurement, and both will ensure that census collection and processing activities remain under control (especially cost control) while maintaining high standards. Nonresponse follow-up, integrated coverage measurement, and the placement of census forms in public places are designed to complement these two main steps by providing mechanisms for maintaining a high-quality census even when address list development and the mail return process understandably fall short of perfection.

Collectively, the procedures are also designed to control costs, partly by increasing quality and thus reducing resource requirements for other aspects of the census process. Efforts to increase the mail return rate, and the use of sampling for nonresponse and vacant dwelling follow-up, have direct implications for reducing the costs of household nonresponse follow-up, which was a major problem in 1990.

Although the panel has expressed various concerns about some details of the Census Bureau's plans (see National Research Council, 1996, 1997b), the panel believes that the basic plans for the 2000 census are sound, based both on the research conducted by the Bureau over the past few years and on its experience from past censuses.

The panel also understands that there are unavoidable operational risks whenever new procedures are introduced in a census. The census is conducted only once every 10 years. There are no other operations sufficiently similar to a full census (particularly with respect to scale) to allow the operationally relevant testing that would ensure that each innovation works well. This is true not only of innovations. It has been demonstrated that one cannot be certain that features used in previous censuses will continue to work effectively in a new census since the nature of society changes, sometimes markedly, over a 10-year span.[4] A key ex-

---

[3]Some states receive these counts earlier.

[4]Waksberg (1998) discusses the history of innovation in the census. As Waksberg mentions, concerns about changes in the census are not new, but innovations have typically succeeded when guided by statistical-based testing and evaluation.

ample involves the inability to predict what proportion of households will mail in their forms as requested, which unexpectedly fell by 10 percentage points from 1980 to 1990, with basically the same methods as in 1980 (National Research Council, 1995). The mail response rate is still a major source of uncertainty in the quality and costs of the 2000 census, despite the use of this procedure for the past several decades.[5]

THE 1998 CENSUS DRESS REHEARSAL AND EVALUATIONS

The last major opportunity to learn about the problems in the census plans is the census dress rehearsal. To acquire information and make final improvements on many aspects of the methodology and operations to be used in carrying out the 2000 census, the Census Bureau will use 37 separate studies based on the 1998 dress rehearsal. (A listing and short description of the 1998 dress rehearsal evaluation studies are given in the appendix to this chapter.) This section lays out the main components and goals of the 1998 census dress rehearsal. No recommendations are offered. The panel concludes that this total evaluation plan will supply a great deal of useful information in making the final decisions regarding the methodology to use in 2000.

The main objective of the dress rehearsal and the associated evaluations is to test the integration of methods in a real-life census environment and to validate plans for the 2000 census. Some evaluations will provide information about the coverage of persons and the quality of the data collected. It is useful to mention that it is impossible for a test census to simulate all aspects of the decennial census for two reasons: the unequaled scale of the decennial census and the public's heightened awareness of it.

In addition, for this dress rehearsal, the decision to test both sampling and nonsampling options limited the opportunity for concentrated effort on one option or the other. A reduction in both sample size and diversity of locations in testing of either approach means that the Census Bureau will be unable to evaluate either approach as comprehensively as was originally planned for the sampling option. Consequently, whichever

---

[5]Early indications from the 1998 dress rehearsal show a 54.1 percent overall mail response rate in South Carolina, 40.6 percent in Menominee, Wisconsin, and 53.7 percent in Sacramento, California. These rates are about 2 percent lower than the 1988 dress rehearsal rates (Bureau of the Census, 1998a). (It should be kept in mind that the 1998 response rates reflect the use of a blanket replacement questionnaire, which was not used in 1988.) The comparable 1990 census rates for these areas were 60 percent for South Carolina and 63 percent for Sacramento: this is not surprising since decennial censuses typically receive greater cooperation than any of their tests or rehearsals.

option is adopted, there is a risk that substantial cost or data quality problems will go undetected.

The dress rehearsal for the 2000 census was conducted at three sites:[6] Sacramento, California; Columbia and 11 surrounding counties in South Carolina; and Menominee County, Wisconsin, which includes the Menominee American Indian Reservation. Both the Sacramento and the South Carolina sites used mailout/mailback for the census enumeration. The South Carolina site also used update leave/mailback for some of the census enumeration in rural areas. At the Sacramento site, sampling for nonresponse follow-up and integrated coverage measurement were used. South Carolina used 100 percent nonresponse follow-up and a post-enumeration survey.[7] The main purpose of this post-enumeration survey was to measure the degree of coverage of the 1990-style census used at that site. The Menominee site used update leave/mailback and 100 percent nonresponse follow-up and tested an integrated coverage measurement program. Since the three sites were not comparable with respect to census processes, the various methods used across sites, specifically in Sacramento and South Carolina, cannot be compared directly. Instead, each site must be evaluated separately.

It is important to point out that the last meeting of this panel took place in June, 1998, when the census dress rehearsal was in its preliminary stages, with very little information available as to the degree of success of various operations.[8] Therefore, the panel cannot offer comments regarding how the results of the dress rehearsal should be used to alter plans for the 2000 census. A new National Research Council panel that has just gotten under way, the Panel to Review the Statistical Procedures of the 2000 Census, is expected to issue an interim report commenting on the dress rehearsal.

The evaluations associated with the census dress rehearsal address eight components of 2000 census methodology: (1) the census questionnaire, (2) construction of the master address file, (3) coverage measure-

---

[6]Much of the following description is from Bureau of the Census (1998a).

[7]By not using sampling for nonresponse follow-up and integrated coverage measurement, the dress rehearsal in South Carolina was meant to approximate the methods used in the 1990 census. However, some of the coverage improvement programs used in 1990 have not been incorporated in this test, which might have made a difference in the coverage of that dress rehearsal at that site.

[8]The recent decision by the U.S. Supreme Court against the use of sampling for use in census counts for purposes of reapportionment was made public while this report was in the last stages of editing and final production. No changes were made to the report as a result of this decision other than the addition of portions of the preface, this footnote, and similar footnotes in the executive summary and in Chapter 2.

ment, (4) coverage improvement, (5) promotion and partnership, (6) unduplication, (7) nonresponse follow-up and field infrastructure, and (8) uses of technology. This section discusses the decisions that face the Census Bureau and how the dress rehearsal is providing information relevant to those decisions. This discussion refers to census dress rehearsal evaluation studies, which are indicated by notation, such as E5, where "E" signifies a type of evaluation study, and "5" indicates the specific study number; these studies are briefly summarized in the appendix to this chapter.

Key Questionnaire-Related Evaluations   With respect to the use of a replacement questionnaire, the key evaluation measurements are the percentage increase in mail response owing to its use and the effects on data quality of undiscovered duplicate responses and the cost of removing the duplicates that are discovered. Also, the percentage of telephone questionnaire assistance calls in which people complained about use of the replacement questionnaire gauges the extent of any negative public reaction. Studies A1 and F1, which provide these measurements, are key in determining whether a nontargeted replacement form should be used in 2000.

Master Address File Evaluations   Three activities assess the completeness and accuracy of the master address file (MAF). First, there is the determination of the number of added addresses received through the Local Update of Census Addresses (LUCA) program.   Second is the determination of the number of additional addresses received as a result of the U.S. Postal Service's casing check.[9]   Finally, a housing unit coverage study, evaluation B1, assesses the completeness and accuracy of the final address list. This study compares the address list with the independent list created in a sample of block clusters for the post-enumeration survey, providing estimates of undercoverage and the frequency of geocoding errors (using dual-system estimation). Evaluation study B2 assesses, also at all three sites, the contribution of each component of the MAF in producing its degree of completeness. Unfortunately, these tests will not evaluate the identical MAF process as planned for the 2000 census: specifically, only a targeted canvass was used, as opposed to the full one planned for 2000.

Coverage Measurement Evaluations   The primary goals at the two major sites with respect to coverage measurement are (1) to measure the

[9]A casing check is a check of the final master address list by Postal Service carriers just prior to Census Day.

net undercount rate for different groups in the South Carolina dress rehearsal site and (2) to determine the extent to which the scheduled milestone dates are met while achieving specified levels of quality at the Sacramento site. Measurement of the net undercount rate in South Carolina
was to determine the potential impact of adjustment for census undercoverage. Examination of the post-enumeration survey schedule in Sacramento helps the Census Bureau understand whether the goal of a "one
number" census was operationally feasible (although the fact that a dress
rehearsal is of a substantially different scale than that of a decennial census complicates the comparison to the timetable of a full decennial census). This is covered by study C1, in Sacramento and Menominee, by
seeing whether scheduled milestone dates for various intermediate steps
are met, whether specified quality levels are met at each milestone, and
what the risk will be of not completing the parallel operations in the 2000
census.

Coverage Improvement Evaluations The key goals at the two
major sites are to determine the success of service-based enumeration, the
"Be Counted" program, and the follow-up of large households.[10] First,
did service-based enumeration add people who would otherwise be
missed using standard housing-unit enumeration? The second goal concerns the "Be Counted" program (covered in evaluation D2) , and the key
measurements are (1) how many people were added through use of the
program, (2) whether they were at addresses that were not on the MAF or
whether they were individuals at otherwise enumerated households, and
(3) how many duplicate enumerations the program generated. Finally,
the effectiveness of the use of the large household follow-up forms in
enumerating households of more than five persons is being measured by
determining the proportion of the mailback universe, by type and household size, that was mailed this form and the resulting response.

Promotion and Partnership Evaluations These evaluations are to
measure any increased awareness of the census through use of paid advertising and the partnership program (a program to enlist the assistance
of local leaders to help increase awareness of the census). An additional
goal is to measure whether the partnership program is effective in mar-
shaling local knowledge and resources to help enumerate local areas.
     Study E1 assesses the effectiveness of paid advertising by measuring
public awareness of the census, the likelihood of completing and returning the census questionnaire, and attitudes that affect this likelihood. To

---

[10]Service-based enumeration is enumeration of the homeless population at places that
offer meals or places to sleep.

evaluate these, a random-digit-dial telephone survey was taken in Sacramento and South Carolina to collect and tabulate responses before and after advertising for comparisons. The partnership program was to be evaluated through examination of contacts with partners and commitments made by partners, as well as by a survey of partners and census field staff. In addition, the level of participation of local and tribal governments in the LUCA program is being assessed.

Unduplication Evaluations   Because there are going to be several opportunities for households to provide more than one census questionnaire in the 2000 census, especially including return of the replacement questionnaire (if used) and "Be Counted" forms, the process of unduplication must be of high quality. These evaluations measure the percentage of erroneous enumerations that resulted from failure to unduplicate multiple responses. In addition, since improper unduplication for forms representing different households results in a census omission, it is important to measure what percentage of census omissions were the result of unduplication rules.

Two key evaluation studies are F1 and F2. Study F1 assesses, at all three dress rehearsal sites, the effectiveness of a computer algorithm, the primary selection algorithm, which selects the persons who are judged to be residents of the housing unit in question, given all of the forms received for that housing unit. A follow-up interview evaluates the quality of the algorithm. In addition, studies F1 and F2 evaluate how often and where duplicates were found and which forms were involved. Study F2 specifically assesses how wide an area should be used to search for duplicate "Be Counted" forms. (Clearly, due to the fact that dress rehearsals are carried out in a very small number of locations, they cannot fully test the ability to identify duplicate responses from geographically disparate areas.)

Nonresponse Follow-Up and Field Infrastructure Evaluations   One of the key variables in carrying out a decennial census is the amount of time necessary to complete field follow-up. The goal of this evaluation was to see if it was possible to hire, train, and maintain staff to conduct nonresponse follow-up. Furthermore, since close-out and last-resort enumerations are presumed to be of lower quality than information collected directly from respondents, and close-out and last-resort enumerations are symptomatic of a census that is running late, it is important to measure the percentage of these proxy enumerations.

Technology-Related Evaluations   These evaluations check specific data capture and data dissemination systems being developed for the

2000 census. They include use of laptop computers for computer-assisted personal interviewing (CAPI) in integrated coverage measurement, optical character recognition technology for data capture, and a sophisticated software system for maintenance of census operations. The questions addressed concern the integration of these systems with more standard census processes and the reliability of the systems.

Summary The census dress rehearsal should give the Census Bureau a greater understanding of key issues: census operations, timing, costs, and logistics; the value of a blanket replacement questionnaire; the ability to hire effective field staff; the operational aspects of integrated coverage measurement, especially the schedule constraints; the use of CAPI instruments and the quality of the data collected; any problems with the census questionnaire; and any problems in developing the master address file.

APPENDIX: CENSUS 2000 DRESS REHEARSAL EVALUATIONS

A. Questionnaire-Related Evaluations [Evaluations A1-A5]. The first group of evaluations deal with issues relating to the various methods of response.

A1. Evaluation of Implementation for Mail Returns. This evaluation addresses issues related to the implementation strategy for delivery of mailbox questionnaires and will provide information about rates and patterns of response. It will also provide information on response rates and completeness of the foreign-language questionnaires. A second component of this evaluation will document if nonresponse follow-up is completed on time and will develop a response profile of nonresponse follow-up units.

A2. Evaluation of the Mail Return Questionnaire. This evaluation focuses on how three components of the mailbox questionnaires affect the quality of the responses: (1) how the paper form is structured, (2) coverage-related questions, and (3) several new or revised content items.

A3. Evaluation of the Short- and Long-Form Simplified Enumerator Questionnaire. The objective of this evaluation is to assess the data quality of the simplified enumerator questionnaire as measured by item nonresponse and patterns of response.

A4. Evaluation of Telephone Questionnaire Assistance. This evaluation has three objectives: (1) to summarize the telephone questionnaire assistance operation, including such information as length of call and reasons for the call; (2) to assess the quality of respondent-provided addresses collected during telephone questionnaire assistance operations; and (3) to determine whether forms mailed out through the telephone questionnaire assistance operation were completed and returned.

A5. Evaluation of the Effect of Alternative Response Options on Long-Form Data. The objective of this evaluation is to determine the frequency with which the alternative response options (telephone questionnaire assistance and "Be Counted" form responses) result in households that were intended to be included in the long-form sample but respond with only short-form data.

B. Master Address File (MAF) Evaluations [Evaluations B1-B2]. There are two evaluations dealing specifically with the MAF.

B1. Evaluation of Housing-Unit Coverage on the MAF. This evaluation addresses how complete the MAF coverage was of housing units at the time of the dress rehearsal enumeration.

B2. Evaluation of the MAF Building Process. The objective of this evaluation is to determine how the various parts of the MAF building process affect the quality and coverage of the MAF.

C. Coverage Measurement Evaluations [Evaluations C1-C8]. These evaluations deal with various aspects of coverage measurement.

C1. Risk Assessment of the Integrated Coverage Measurement Field Data Collection and Processing Schedule of Operations. This evaluation will measure conformance to the overall schedule and intermediate milestones, as well as the effects on data collection and processing completeness and quality.

C2. Contamination of Initial Phase Data Collected in Integrated Coverage Measurement Block Clusters. The purpose of this study is to determine if integrated coverage measurement (ICM) affects census results.

C3. Evaluation of Outmover Tracing and Interviewing. Whole-household outmover tracing will be evaluated at the site level as well as for different populations based on the poststrata used.

C4. Error Profile for the Census 2000 Dress Rehearsal. The first aspect of the error profile is to examine individually the sources of error corresponding to the enumeration process that are measurable and feasible to measure given the design of the Census 2000 Dress Rehearsal Integrated Coverage Measurement Survey. The second aspect of the error profile is to examine the net effect of a subset of these sources of error by estimating a net nonsampling error and combining it with the sampling, or random, error.

C5. Evaluation of Quality Assurance Falsification Model for Integrated Coverage Measurement Personal Interview. The goal of this evaluation is to measure the efficiency and effectiveness of the falsification reports and the operations used to implement the model.

C6. Evaluation of the Integrated Coverage Measurement/Post-Enumeration Survey Personal Follow-Up Interview. The purpose of this evaluation is to identify potential problems with question wording and ordering and other questionnaire design issues in the personal follow-up interviews.

C7. Assessment of Consistency of Census Estimates with Demographic Benchmarks. This study represents an extension of the demographic analysis program that the Census Bureau has used for many years to evaluate the consistency of census results and the completeness of coverage at the national level. It uses independent demographic benchmarks to evaluate (1) the consistency of the dress rehearsal census estimates and (2) the effectiveness of integrated coverage measurement in achieving a reduction in the differential undercount.

C8. Analysis of the Final Numbers and Estimates. This evaluation contains five separate research projects under one heading. It can be thought of as the research umbrella for projects whose focus is improvements to and refinements of the sampling and estimation methodology for the 2000 census. The five research projects are raking evaluation, evaluation of bias from integrated coverage measurement missing data methodology, heterogeneity/small-area estimation evaluation, household-level data file research, and mover estimation evaluation.

D. Coverage Improvement Evaluations [Evaluations D1-D5]. These evaluations provide information on various programs intended to improve person coverage in the census. Both the service-based enumeration and the "Be Counted" program are intended to include people in the census who may be missed in the standard housing unit and group quarters enumerations.

D1. Service-Based Enumeration Coverage Yield Evaluation. This evaluation documents the coverage of persons included in the dress rehearsal as a result of the service-based enumeration program.

D2. Evaluation Study of the "Be Counted" Program. This evaluation documents the coverage of persons included in the dress rehearsal as a result of the "Be Counted" program.

D3. Evaluation of the Coverage Edit Operation. This evaluation will provide data on the appropriateness of the coverage edit rules and on the effectiveness of the edits and the follow-up.

D4. Evaluation of the Large-Household Follow-Up. This evaluation will provide data on the effectiveness of mailing a follow-up form to complete the enumeration of households with more than five persons.

D5. Coverage Improvement Uses for Administrative Records in a Nonsample Census. The objective of this evaluation is to determine if coverage in a nonsample census can be improved by using data from administrative records. There are three components to this evaluation: file acquisition, coverage research, and field follow-up.

E. Promotion Evaluation [Evaluation E1]. There is just one evaluation about promotion.

E1. Effectiveness of Paid Advertising. This evaluation will answer the question "Does public awareness about dress rehearsal activities increase as a result of paid advertising, and what does this tell us about the success of the paid advertising campaign?"

F. Multiple-Response Resolution Evaluations [Evaluations F1-F3]. Because the options for responding to the census have increased since 1990, it is critical to develop a system for unduplicating multiple responses. This group of evaluations will provide information that will be used to refine the multiple response resolution process for the 2000 census.

F1. Evaluation Study of the Primary Selection Algorithm. The objective here is to evaluate the process of unduplicating multiple returns for the same address. For one component of this evaluation, an independent interview will be conducted at addresses for which more than one census form was returned to determine if specific rules were appropriate in determining the correct residents of the households. From the independent interview, erroneous enumerations will be calculated and omission rates for the specific rules evaluated. There is an operational component that will document the process used in the primary selection algorithm. The third component is to determine the operational effectiveness of the dress rehearsal invalid-return detection operation in identifying geographically clustered invalid returns.

F2. Evaluation Study of the Within-Block Search Operation. This evaluation will simulate the within-block search operation by adding additional forms to the search and extending the search area to surrounding blocks. Similar to F1, there is an operational component to F2 to quantify the effect of the within-block search.

F3. Evaluation Study of Intentional Fraud. Contractor-provided returns are used to determine if the plan for multiple-response resolution is successful in identifying and eliminating invalid returns.

G. Nonresponse Follow-up and Field Infrastructure Evaluations [Evaluations G1-G10]. Group G evaluations provide information about the implementation of the field operations and various aspects of the field infrastructure. They are designed to answer a wide range of questions.

G1. Ability to Fully Staff Each Operation. Was the Census Bureau able to hire, train, and maintain staff to execute nonresponse follow-up, integrated coverage measurement, and the post-enumeration survey? This evaluation is closely tied to G4 (pay rates) and G8 (recruiting activities).

G2. Field Infrastructure: Job Requirements. What are the essential job functions and physical demands for local census office positions? This identification will be necessary in designing accommodations under the Rehabilitation Act of 1973 and Americans with Disabilities Act. This evaluation will also help document the appropriateness of selection factors used in hiring, such as access to a car.

G3. Field Infrastructure: Criterion Validation. Are there significant correlations between applicants' selection-aid test scores and measures of their job performance in terms of enumerator production rates, attendance, and length of stay?

G4. Field Infrastructure: Pay Rates. Were staff members able to be hired and maintained to execute the nonresponse follow-up using the pay rates from an economic model developed by Westat, Inc. (a contractor for the census), and the Census Bureau?

G5. Field Infrastructure: Preappointment Management System/Automated Decennial Administrative Management System. Do these systems work? An enterprise-wide integrated system will perform applicant processing and selection, personnel action processing, payroll processing, and history and reporting: How will it interface with other census systems?

G6. Field Infrastructure: Supply Ordering Process. Was the Census Bureau able to provide enough supplies for all aspects of the dress rehearsal?

G7. Field Infrastructure: Equal Employment Opportunity (EEO) Process. Does the EEO Program set up for the dress rehearsal (a new automated system) adequately track complaints? Does it ensure that specific tasks related to a complaint are completed? Does it lead to a possible resolution of the complaint?

G8. Field Infrastructure: Recruiting Activities. Were the Census Bureau's recruiting activities successful? Which specific sources of applicants were the best? Were the activities done at the right time? What advertising sources were most effective? What did it cost?

G9. Field Infrastructure: Welfare to Work. Did the Census Bureau's dress rehearsal Welfare to Work Program work? That is, how well were census recruiters and partnership specialists able to identify state, local, and tribal government resources, as well as community resources, to aid in the development of an applicant pool of welfare recipients?

G10. Enumerator Training for Nonresponse Follow-Up and Integrated Coverage Measurement Personal Interview. Did the training provided to enumerators result in skilled employees able to perform at an acceptable level?

H. Technology-Related Evaluations [Evaluations H1 and H3]. Results of Group H evaluations will be used for internal Census Bureau planning to validate specific data capture systems being developed for the 2000 census.

H1. Evaluation of Segmented Write-ins. This evaluation will analyze respondents' use of the segmented boxes on the questionnaires for race and ethnicity.

H2. H2 has been dropped.

H3. Quality of the Data Capture System. This evaluation will look at what percentage of the answers in the dress rehearsal database are different from the actual responses on the census questionnaires.

2

Census Methodology

This chapter summarizes the panel's most recent findings concerning the six new processes proposed for introduction in the 2000 census and described in Chapter 1: (1) master address file development, (2) efforts to enhance the mail return rate, (3) availability of "Be Counted" forms in public places, (4) sampling for nonresponse follow-up, (5) integrated coverage measurement, and (6) statistical estimation.

MASTER ADDRESS FILE DEVELOPMENT

In its second interim report (National Research Council, 1997b), the panel reiterated the importance of a high-quality address list for the 2000 census. One way to improve the quality of the 2000 census relative to the 1990 census while reducing costs is to make the master address file (MAF) more complete than it was in 1990. The collection of high-quality data for small geographic areas is greatly facilitated through the use of an address list of uniformly high quality for the entire nation. A poor address list can contribute greatly to increased rates and poor estimates of the rates of census omissions and erroneous enumerations, including duplicates. Also, to increase the level of confidence in decennial census procedures, local stakeholders—officials, business leaders, interest group representatives—must be convinced that the address lists for the 2000 census are better than the 1990 lists for their areas.

To improve the MAF, the Census Bureau has made use of updates from the U.S. Postal Service and has solicited input from local officials. The Census Bureau recognizes, however, that these efforts have not been as effective as initially hoped. Information received from the Postal Service has not been timely, and a greater proportion of the country remains without city-style postal addresses than was anticipated. At the same time, it has become clear that a substantial number of local authorities lack the resources to provide timely updates of address information of adequate quality in a usable format (i.e., referenced to the correct location on census block boundary maps). Therefore, the Census Bureau has decided that it will implement a nationwide check of addresses immediately prior to the 2000 census, although this additional check will be costly. The panel strongly endorses this change in plans.

EFFORTS TO ENHANCE THE MAIL RETURN RATE

The Census Bureau conducted systematic research early in the 1990s to identify procedures that would increase the proportion of households that return their census form by mail (see National Research Council, 1994). The research indicated that mail response rates would likely increase, relative to 1990, as a result of (1) improvements in the design of census envelopes and forms, (2) the use of prenotification letters, (3) clear information about the mandatory nature of the census, and (4) sending nonrespondents a reminder notice and then a replacement questionnaire. Tests and other research indicate that the resulting reduction in the need for nonresponse follow-up will more than offset the increase in census costs from these changes.

In the development work and testing carried out before the dress rehearsal, replacement forms had been sent only to households that did not return the original form by a specified date. In developing operations for the 2000 census, the Census Bureau has learned that the scale of the decennial census and timing constraints will not permit the mailing of replacement forms only to nonrespondent households (a targeted replacement questionnaire). Instead, replacement questionnaires must be mailed to all households on the MAF (a blanket replacement questionnaire). This nontargeted mailing of replacement questionnaires to all households was tested for the first time in the 1998 census dress rehearsal. While early indications were that the second mailout significantly increased response rates in the test,[1] there was also a considerable amount of duplication. Therefore, the panel remains concerned that mailing replacement forms to all households could generate millions of duplicate submissions in 2000, which the Bureau must identify and exclude, as well as reduce

---

[1]Increases were from 47.2 to 55.4 percent (up 8.2 percent) for areas using the mailout/mailback methodology in South Carolina and from 46.1 to 53.7 percent (up 7.6 percent) for Sacramento (Bureau of the Census, 1998b).

cooperation by creating an impression of wastefulness and by increasing respondent burden. The generation of millions of duplicate forms will likely result in delays for later census operations and additional errors. It is therefore critical that thorough evaluation of this procedure follow the 1998 census dress rehearsal on a schedule that allows the findings to influence plans for the 2000 census.[2]

SAMPLING FOR NONRESPONSE FOLLOW-UP

In its first and second interim reports (National Research Council, 1996, 1997b), the panel endorsed using sampling, combined with statistical estimation, to efficiently and effectively collect information on households that do not respond by mail or to other opportunities for enumeration. The panel expects that a properly designed and well-executed sampling plan for nonresponse follow-up can save more than $100 million (assuming a sampling rate of 75 percent, see Brown et al., 1998) and possibly increase the quality of the census data collected by enumerators.

The likely improvement in quality has both direct and indirect aspects. Directly, by reducing the total workload, sampling for nonresponse follow-up will allow for improvements in the control and management of field operations that in turn would lead to an increase in the quality of the census data collected by enumerators. Indirectly, the nonresponse follow-up interviews of a sample of nonrespondents can be completed in a more timely fashion than follow-up of all nonrespondents, which will lead to improvements in quality in the integrated coverage measurement operation.

It is important to point out that given the overall sampling rate of roughly 70 percent (depending on the 2000 mail-return rate), the benefits gained through greater control and management of field operations and the completion of the field work more expeditiously are substantially limited in comparison with what would be gained with a more typical (lower) rate of sampling. However, as argued in Chapter 3, the panel agrees with the Census Bureau's more conservative approach to this planned, initial use of sampling for nonresponse follow-up in the decennial census. Given the sampling rate, it is difficult to argue for large, simultaneous benefits both in time saved and in field control and management.

In its second interim report (National Research Council, 1997b), the panel strongly endorsed the Census Bureau's switch to an approach re-

---

[2]The panel issued a letter report on November 10, 1997, discussing the possible problems resulting from the use of a blanket replacement questionnaire (National Research Council, 1997a).

ferred to as direct sampling, in which the mailout/mailback phase is followed directly by nonresponse follow-up on a sample basis, with no intermediate period of 100 percent nonresponse follow-up. The panel expressed concern that the sampling rates proposed at that time would result in coefficients of variation that were too high in areas with high primary response rates, in comparison with other areas. The Census Bureau has since modified the sampling plan for nonresponse follow-up so that census tracts with primary response rates of more than 85 percent will be sampled at a rate of 1 in 3. That rate, combined with the planned sampling rates for areas with lower initial response rates, means that most areas will have similar levels of sampling error. Should any tracts achieve an initial response rate of more than 95 percent, they will have somewhat lower levels of sampling error than the rest of the country.

The panel strongly endorses this most recent change in sampling rates for nonresponse follow-up. The overall nonresponse follow-up sampling plan now is more efficient, and the field work will be easier to control. Given no unanticipated operational problems, all census tracts will be enumerated with high reliability with respect to nonresponse follow-up.

One concern that has been expressed about the plan to use sampling for nonresponse follow-up is that it could lead to results with relatively high levels of sampling error for areas with small populations. While the panel addressed this issue in its first and second interim reports, we now provide additional detail. It is also useful to point out that this concern has been greatly alleviated because the sampling rate will be a minimum of 1 in 3 for all census tracts and will likely be considerably higher in most of the country. Thus, assuming a mail response rate of 65 percent, the Census Bureau will be following up approximately 25 million nonresponding households in 6 weeks.

The Census Bureau recognizes that the use of sampling for nonresponse follow-up will introduce sampling errors in essentially each census block. The estimation procedures to be used in conjunction with sampling for nonresponse follow-up use information from sampled households to project results for nonsampled households from the same block, to the extent feasible. Inevitably, those who are included in the sample will differ from those who are not, so that the results obtained from the sample data will include some error.[3] However, the scientific sampling procedure that the Census Bureau proposes, known as stratified probability sampling, yields counts with three important properties

---

[3]Throughout this report the term "error" is used in its statistical meaning to denote the difference between an estimate and the true value.

with regard to these errors. First, the error in any one block is not systematic or predictable in its direction. In particular, the direction of the sampling error cannot be manipulated to reach a predetermined outcome in a given area. Second, the range of possible estimates derived from a sample can be determined reliably for any level of geography. Third, the relative size of these sampling errors decreases as the size of the population in the area increases.

Furthermore, the results from using sampling in this way could lead to more accurate counts (depending on the size of the area) because errors from the amount of proxy enumeration in the census will probably be reduced and therefore the data that are collected could be of higher quality. In this context, it is important to realize that every recent decennial census has had a considerable amount of proxy response. The less intense and uneven quality of past efforts to collect data from initial non-respondents with 100 percent nonresponse follow-up resulted in the collection of poorer quality data, particularly because of relatively high rates for proxy enumeration[4] than would be achieved with a sample-based nonresponse follow-up. With sampling for nonresponse follow-up, the extent of proxy response could be considerably reduced, at the cost of adding sampling variability, which diminishes quickly with increasing population size.

Consider an area 25 times the size of a census tract, i.e., roughly 40,000 housing units,[5] a level of census geography well below that of a congressional district. (In this calculation we ignore the likely modest benefits from stratification that the Census Bureau is planning on using, which would make the argument stronger.) To take the worst case with respect to the nonresponse sampling rate, assume this area has a mailback rate of 85 percent (and therefore a nonresponse sampling rate of 1 in 3), and that there are a mean number of 2.5 people per housing unit (100,000 people in all) and a standard deviation of 1.5 people per housing unit. The standard error of the average number of people per housing unit due to sampling for nonresponse follow-up would be approximately .027, and the standard error on the total population would be 162. Now assume that nonresponse follow-up would miss (or overcount) 500 of the 15,000 people to be followed up, or 3.33 percent. Then sampling for nonresponse

---

[4]The two proxy methods are last-resort and closeout enumeration. Last-resort enumeration is the collection of data from neighbors, apartment managers, USPS employees, etc., and is used when a response from a resident cannot be obtained. Closeout enumeration is the use of whatever data have been collected by the date by which all interviewing must be concluded, with imputation used to fill in any missing information.

[5]Housing units include units that might be vacant; occupied housing units contain households.

follow-up would have lower mean square error (and be preferred) if it missed less than 3.15 percent of the 5,000 people followed up—if it missed less than 158 out of 5,000 (rather than 167 without sampling). Since the workload is reduced from 6,000 to 2,000 households, this seems quite feasible.

For another example, assume that the mail return rate is 65 percent, the standard error for the total population is 112, and nonresponse follow-up again has an error of 500, this time in counting the 35,000 non-responding people for a miss rate of 1.43 percent. Sampling for non-response follow-up, in counting 25,000 people, would have lower mean square error if it missed (less than or equal to) 348 of these 25,000 for a miss rate of 1.39 percent (rather than 357 without sampling). This again seems like a feasible gain given the reduction in workload from 14,000 to 10,000 households. Finally, we point out that it is certainly arguable that rushing nonresponse follow-up could increase the error rate since the average rate for closeout and last-resort enumeration for the 1990 census was 3.5 percent, and the erroneous enumeration rate for these cases was around 40 percent (Ericksen et al., 1991).

We now add to the above argument the possible reduction in the number of movers and errors caused by movers through the more rapid completion of nonresponse follow-up through use of sampling. On the basis of this evidence and reasoning, the panel believes that the results from sampling for nonresponse follow-up will be of equal or better quality than would result from the continuation of the procedures used in 1990 when used for important purposes, such as delineating congressional districts, and that for other uses of census data, sampling for nonresponse follow-up at the very least approximately replicates what would be obtained, in terms of data quality, with 100 percent follow-up. It is useful to point out that many problems will be common to follow-up regardless of whether or not sampling is used. People's attitudes towards being enumerated, their work schedule, and ease of access to residences are the same, whether sampling is used or not.

Finally, there are some valid concerns about the implementation of various administrative operations with this first application of such a large, time-constrained sample survey. One worry is what difficulties may result from the constraint to produce a "one-number" census, and whether this may result in time-abbreviated nonresponse follow-up or integrated coverage measurement. The dress rehearsal is a key for understanding what implementation issues need to be addressed before 2000.

Concern has also been expressed that sampling for nonresponse follow-up presents an opportunity for political manipulation. Such manipulation is simply impossible. In addition to the enormous complexity of any manipulation, the constraint that the census methodology be prespecified, a requirement that the Census Bureau is strictly observing, would make identification of any manipulation easy. At this time, many of the details concerning sample design and estimation are currently fixed for the 2000 census; for a few important issues yet to be resolved, their resolution depends primarily on results from the 1998 census dress rehearsal. Also, the estimation for sampling for nonresponse follow-up is simple and has been prespecified (except for the treatment of late responses, for which a procedure has been suggested and will be decided on well before the census).

To manipulate sampling for nonresponse follow-up at the design stage, someone at the Census Bureau would have to know which of the more than 30 million mail nonrespondent households had more or fewer residents and then manipulate the computer-generated random-number-based selection of households for follow-up so that the households in a particular area that were included in the sample were on average larger or smaller. This is, of course, unimaginable.

Furthermore, sampling does not provide additional opportunities for manipulation in the field. Without sampling an enumerator would visit the nonrespondents on a certain block. With sampling the same enumerator would simply visit a subset of the same nonrespondents. An enumerator would have no idea whether sampling was occurring on a particular block (sampling would not be used on integrated coverage measurement blocks) since the enumerator would not know whether an address was skipped because it was not in the sample or because a response had already been received by mail. Finally, it is important to state in response to this concern that the Census Bureau, except for a handful of top management positions, is staffed by career civil servants who have a long-standing reputation for integrity and professionalism.

INTEGRATED COVERAGE MEASUREMENT

Both because the master address list, despite the Census Bureau's best efforts, is incomplete and because individuals who live in otherwise enumerated households are at times missed, all decennial censuses fail to count everyone. In addition, due to people moving, having more than one residence, and confusion as to the census definition of residence, many individuals are counted more than once or are counted erroneously. The net effect of undercoverage and overcoverage is referred to as net undercoverage. This net undercoverage affects some groups and geographic areas more than others—that is, the census has *differential* (net) undercoverage. For example, for 1990 the net undercount of black males aged 25 to 54 was measured by demographic analysis to have been around 12 percent (see Robinson et al., 1993), compared with a net undercount of non-black males 25 to 54 that was estimated to be around 3 percent. In 1990, again as estimated by demographic analysis for blacks, the largest undercounted group for females was children 0 to 9 years old (Robinson et al., 1993), for whom the undercount was around 8.0 percent. Since the differential net undercoverage has persisted for some demographic groups, especially blacks, over several censuses, these groups have been consistently underrepresented in census figures, resulting in possible misallocations of political representation and government funds.[6]

Dual-System Estimation

The decennial censuses from 1950 through 1990 all made use of various evaluation programs to assess the extent of gross and net census undercoverage and its causes. (For a description of these programs and their findings, see National Research Council, 1985; Hogan, 1992.) The only methodology that has been shown to be feasible to measure the amount of differential undercoverage at relatively low levels of geographic aggregation is a large-scale post-enumeration survey with dual-system estimation. (This is the approach planned for use in the 2000 census and referred to in that context as integrated coverage measurement.)

The basic statistical model represented by the term dual-system estimation (ignoring some complications) is as follows. A first enumeration, the census, is carried out, followed by a second enumeration, the post-enumeration survey. Those enumerated by both processes are identified through matching the two lists of those enumerated each time. A key assumption used in this model is that the probability of enumeration in the second process given enumeration in the first process is identical to the probability of enumeration in the second process given a miss in the first process. This is equivalent to the assumption that the events of enumeration in the first and second processes are statistically independent. This assumed identity provides a basis for estimating the number that were not enumerated with either process, and therefore the total population.[7] This method was originally proposed by Sekar and Deming

---

[6]When considering geographic areas, it is important to recognize that net undercoverage for an area is a mixture of the rates of undercoverage of the demographic groups represented in an area, weighted by the count of each group.

[7]Dual-system estimation is based on the following argument (separately conducted in several poststrata) to estimate the total population size, denoted DSE. Let Cen be the number of persons enumerated in the census, N_p be the number of persons enumerated in the post-enumeration survey, and M be the number enumerated in both, established by matching one with the other. Then the independence assumption equates the probability of

(1949), who coined the term dual-system estimation (DSE). In addition to the fact that DSE depends on the important assumption that the events of inclusion in the census and in the post-enumeration survey are independent, it is also important that there be an appropriate random sampling scheme that chooses blocks for inclusion in the post-enumeration survey so that inferences from the sampled blocks extend to the unsampled ones. (The Census Bureau goes to great lengths to ensure this.) Finally, since the probabilities of inclusion in the census and in the post-enumeration survey are known to depend on various characteristics of members of the population, post-stratification is typically used to produce subgroups for which these probabilities are more homogeneous (see below).

DSE was the methodology used in 1980 and 1990 to join information from the post-enumeration survey and the census to measure census undercoverage. In the 1990 census, a post-enumeration survey of roughly 160,000 housing units collected information to measure the amount of under- and overcoverage in the census, along with other characteristics of those persons who were missed or erroneously enumerated.

In 1980 and 1990 the problem of differential undercoverage was addressed exclusively in the official counts through the use of coverage improvement programs. These programs (e.g., the nonhousehold sources check[8]) were used to try to increase the coverage of historically undercounted groups. Not only were many of these programs generally unsuccessful, they tended to be expensive, costing as much as $76 (in 1980 dollars) per added person in the 1980 census (see National Research Council, 1985). Furthermore, Ericksen et al. (1991) and Griffin and Moriarity (1992) showed that in the 1990 census these programs often added a substantial number of erroneous enumerations. (There was a direct relationship between the amount of erroneous additions and the distance from census day.) Therefore, the use of coverage improvement programs alone is unlikely to be effective in greatly reducing differential undercoverage.

---

enumeration in the post-enumeration survey, estimated by N_p/DSE with the probability of enumeration in the post-enumeration survey given enumeration in the census, estimated by M/Cen. Algebra then equates DSE to $[Np][Cen]/M$, and the estimate follows. To accommodate the complications due to inclusion of the contributions of imputations (II) and erroneous enumerations (EE), and census enumerations (N_e) as measured for the post-enumeration survey areas, we get:

$$DSE = N_p \left(\frac{Cen - II}{M} \right) \left(1 - \frac{EE}{N_e} \right).$$

[8]The nonhousehold sources check was used in areas with large minority populations. Census Bureau district office staff conducted a clerical match between census records and drivers' license records, immigration records, and (in New York City) welfare records. The addresses of nonmatched individuals were then visited by enumerators.

A successful application of integrated coverage measurement has the advantage of greatly reducing the need for expensive and ineffective coverage improvement programs. Furthermore, as mentioned above, the elimination of unsuccessful coverage improvement programs reduces the rate of erroneous enumerations, which can reduce the error in integrated coverage measurement, and it may provide more time for integrated coverage measurement.

Finally, as we have noted, sampling for nonresponse follow-up has the promise of being able to conclude nonresponse follow-up more expeditiously. This, in turn, would permit the integrated coverage measurement survey interviewers to begin work earlier, which will reduce the number of individuals who have moved since the census, which will reduce the number of erroneous enumerations due to people being enumerated a second time at an address other than the census day address. Thus, overall, sampling for nonresponse follow-up will increase the quality of the information collected in integrated coverage measurement, which will facilitate matching, one of the major concerns arising with the use of integrated coverage measurement.

Response to Arguments Against
Integrated Coverage Measurement

The panel is well aware of the controversy involving the proposed use of sampling in the 2000 census for nonresponse follow-up and for integrated coverage measurement. This final report presents an opportunity for the panel to comment on the controversy. The public debate surrounding sampling in the census has often confused the use of sampling for nonresponse follow-up and sampling as part of integrated coverage measurement. As argued above, the two activities interact, but they are different applications of sampling and target different problems in the census. This section first notes some arguments that have been given against sampling in the census in general and against sampling for nonresponse follow-up in particular. This is followed by an introduction to the leading technical criticisms of integrated coverage measurement ("adjustment" in 1990 terminology), which are treated in more depth in Chapter 4.

One argument against sampling for nonresponse follow-up concerns the possible manipulation of the results. We address the concern above; it is completely unfounded. Since sampling for nonreponse follow-up is a routine application of standard sampling techniques and practices, it is generally not subjected to *technical* criticism aside from the specific design and possible operational complications, except as a criticism of the addition of sampling variability to counts for areas, as discussed above (and possibly as a criticism of the estimation used in conjunction with late returns). However, a nontechnical criticism has been expressed that sampling in the census, especially for nonresponse follow-up, ignores the constitutional requirement for a complete enumeration of the nation's population. The panel recognizes that a decennial census is constitutionally linked to the apportionment of political representation among the states, legally linked to the distribution of many types of federal funds, and used as a basis for forming congressional districts within states to conform to constitutional requirements. These links are the root of legal and constitutional debates about the census. They are rightly settled by the courts. The panel makes no attempt to anticipate judicial rulings on what restrictions on methods, if any, are implied by the Constitution and relevant legislation. The panel takes as its premise that the most accurate counts and shares are sought at the various levels for which they are needed in a cost-effective manner and that systematic and persistent errors are particularly problematic.

The panel notes, though, that census questionnaires or enumerators are sent to all the households with addresses on the MAF, which have an opportunity to respond. In addition, there are a variety of respondent-friendly opportunities for enumeration by telephone and mail. Sampling comes into play only for housing units from which no response is obtained from the initial mailout (or visit in nonmailout/mailback areas). We reiterate our conclusion that sampling for nonresponse follow-up is an excellent technical way to control census costs and potentially improve quality.

Chapter 4 focuses on technical arguments concerning the use of sampling in the census as part of integrated coverage measurement. The following issues are addressed there: (1) matching error and the bias from imputation of match status for unresolved cases, (2) unmodeled heterogeneity in census undercoverage for lower levels of geographic aggregation (violation of the so-called synthetic assumption), and (3) correlation bias, focusing on the heterogeneity of probabilities of enumeration of individuals in the census and in the integrated coverage measurement survey. Chapter 4 examines the studies of matching error, explores the synthetic assumption, and discusses the problem of correlation bias.

Finally, with respect to court decisions on sampling in the census, the panel is aware that there have been two recent decisions against the use of sampling to produce the counts that will be used to reapportion the U.S. House of Representatives after the 2000 census. If these decisions are upheld by the U.S. Supreme Court,[9] it will not be possible to use sam-

---

[9]The recent decision by the U.S. Supreme Court on January 25, 1999, that sampling cannot be used to collect census counts for purposes of congressional reapportionment was

pling for nonresponse follow- up as part of the 2000 census. However, "adjusted" counts can be produced in addition to "traditional" census counts. Therefore, while the restriction not to use sampling for apportionment would prohibit the use of adjusted counts for apportionment, it would still be possible to benefit from integrated coverage measurement for many other important uses of census data, such as allocation of federal and state funds to states and localities. Also, for these purposes, the adjusted counts are not needed by December 31, 2000. Of course, the situation would not be the same as originally planned for integrated coverage measurement, in which there is one set of official estimates. In this case there may be two sets of estimates—one that makes no use of sampling and another that uses the integrated coverage measurement estimates of all areas.

The importance of the many uses of small-area census data argues strongly for retention of the current plans for the integrated coverage measurement survey as a sample of 750,000 housing units. This sample size may enhance public acceptance of census results since it permits making estimates for states directly without the need to use information from other states. In turn, estimates for substate areas, which are used for many program administration, planning, and research purposes, can be based on information specific to each state. Therefore, the panel strongly supports the large-scale integrated coverage measurement survey as planned for the 2000 census.

STATISTICAL ESTIMATION

The panel examined one statistical estimation issue:[10] how to assign the persons added through the integrated coverage measurement survey to households when all that is known about them are their demographic characteristics and some geographic information at a relatively high level.[11] If information on census undercoverage had been used for offi-

---

made public while this report was in the last stages of editing and final production. No changes were made to the report as a result of this decision other than the addition of portions of the preface, this footnote, and similar footnotes in Chapter 1 and the executive summary.

[10]The estimation issue of what to do about the delivery of late mail returns was presented to the panel too late to be addressed in this report. However, this is an important issue that should be examined for potential bias.

[11]This problem is not faced in sampling for nonresponse follow-up since there the imputation is done on a household basis, whereas in integrated coverage measurement the characteristics are determined on an individual basis. However, in integrated coverage measurement, the people counted in the post-enumeration survey but missed in the census do have a household affiliation based on the post-enumeration survey interview, but this information is not used in providing household characteristics of the undercounted population.

cial purposes in 1990, there was no statistically satisfactory way of assigning household characteristics to the added persons. Files for people included through adjustment would have been added to the census data files by imputing individuals from the appropriate poststrata. These individuals' housing types would have been listed as special quarters, that is, they would not have been placed in distinct households.

For the 2000 census the Census Bureau initiated a research project early in the 1990s to determine if something more effective could be done. Specifically, the Bureau examined the creation of a so-called transparent file in which all of the additions obtained through use of integrated coverage measurement would be incorporated into the distribution of households and thus be transparent to data users.[12] The Bureau's initial plan would have altered the relative weighting of larger versus smaller households in order to obtain the desired counts of persons by demographic characteristics. Thus for example, three-person households with certain characteristics might be increased while two-person households with otherwise similar characteristics were reduced.

The initial procedure presented by the Census Bureau raised a concern for the panel. The panel's views were informed by other research in this general area (see Zaslavsky, 1988; Zanutto and Zaslavsky, 1996). However, no other approach had been demonstrated to be feasible in a large-scale production setting. It is our understanding that recent advances to the initial procedure may have addressed the panel's concern. But because the Census Bureau's decision on whether to integrate this into the production operation had to be made on the basis of the performance of the initial procedure, the panel understands the decision to essentially repeat the method of the 1990 census, i.e., persons added through use of integrated coverage measurement will be assigned for their household, to the special quarters category. Especially given the limited time for evaluation of statistical models, this seems to be a reasonable decision for 2000. However, the panel strongly supports the Bureau's intention to produce the transparent file at a later date.

---

[12]The transparent file and other data products based on it would have no flags or indicators of which household records resulted from imputations and which household records were directly collected from respondents. This makes sense since the fact that some households are replicated and some dropped using this methodology makes the notion of an imputation not clearly applicable.

3

Reconsideration of Important Census Bureau Decisions

The planning of a decennial census begins at least 10 years before the first questionnaire is mailed out. Some decisions must be made relatively early in the decade, for example, because of the need to procure equipment or because of limited testing opportunities. While the panel supports the fundamental decisions that the Census Bureau has made in planning for the 2000 census regarding the use of sampling for nonresponse follow-up and integrated coverage measurement, various decisions that the Census Bureau was required to make early in the 1990s that cannot be changed until the 2010 census planning cycle—some supported and some not supported by this panel—need to be revisited for 2010. (One important reason for reconsidering many of these decisions is technical and methodological advances that are either likely or expected before the next census.) This should be done with the benefit of evaluation results and data collected from 2000.

This chapter discusses the following features involved in these decisions, some of which will be used in 2000 and some not, in roughly the chronological order of their appearance in the census process:

- the decision to carry out a full master address file canvass prior to the census;
- the decision not to move census day;
- the use of multiple response opportunities;
- the use of blanket replacement questionnaires;
- the use of four sampling rates for the long form (assuming use of the long form in 2010);

- the use of the sampling rate chosen for undeliverable-as-addressed vacant housing units;
- the obligation to use nonresponse follow-up to directly enumerate at least 90 percent of households in combination with mail response;
- the restriction to use at least a 1-in-3 sampling rate in areas of high mail response;
- the use of hot deck imputation for nonresponse follow-up and vacant households;
- the use of computer-assisted personal interviewing for integrated coverage measurement;
- the treatment of missing data in integrated coverage measurement;
- issues involving use of dual-system estimation;
- the decision not to combine demographic analysis with integrated coverage measurement;
- the prohibition against using integrated coverage measurement estimates that borrow information across states;
- the use of "raking" rather than more complex modeling for small-area estimation from dual-system estimation; and
- the creation of a transparent household file.

A FULL MASTER ADDRESS FILE CANVASS

A complete master address file is crucial to a 2000 census that produces reliable small-area tabulations. In addition, the MAF needs to be referenced to the correct geographic location in the computerized census feature maps, referred to as the Topologically Integrated Geographic Encoding and Referencing (TIGER) system. The completeness and accuracy of the geographically referenced address list (MAF-TIGER) is important to provide adequate support for key data collection operations planned for the 2000 census:

- mailout and postal delivery of the census questionnaires for mail-back return;
- census delivery of questionnaires for mailback return in rural areas;
- unduplication of multiple questionnaire responses from the same household, which results from multiple response options and mailout of replacement questionnaires; and
- enumerator field follow-up for nonresponse, including accurate sampling to achieve 90 percent direct enumeration in each census tract.

To assure a high-quality MAF-TIGER, the Census Bureau has undertaken initiatives throughout the 1990s to keep these files up to date. At the national level, the Bureau has partnered with the U.S. Postal Service

(USPS) to make regular updates to the MAF based on the USPS delivery sequence file (DSF). The DSF provides a nationwide source for identifying new addresses to add to the MAF as originally developed for the 1990 census, including both addresses not included on the 1990 address list as well as addresses new from 1990. At the subnational level, the Census Bureau has partnered with local governments through the Tiger Improvement Program and the Program for Address List Supplementation (PALS) to identify the street location of new addresses added to the MAF and to supplement MAF improvements based on the DSF.

As late as spring 1997, the Census Bureau anticipated that these efforts, combined with targeted field canvassing in urban areas[1] and blanket field canvassing of rural areas would be sufficient to build a high quality MAF-TIGER for conducting the 2000 census. In its second interim report (National Research Council, 1997b), the panel stated that the Census Bureau had not demonstrated that it could effectively identify where the MAF-TIGER was deficient and then correct the deficiencies through targeted updating checks. By late summer 1997 the Bureau's internal evaluation determined that the national partnership with the USPS using the DSF file and the local partnership programs, in conjunction with targeted canvassing, would not produce the high-quality MAF-TIGER needed to conduct the 2000 census. Specifically, the DSF file missed too many addresses for new construction and was not updated at the same rate across all areas of the country (for details, see U.S. General Accounting Office, 1998). The PALS local government partnership program failed because of the poor response of local governments (often based on lack of resources) and the Census Bureau's inability to anticipate, make sense of, and process the various submissions (both paper and electronic) received from local governments.

In September 1997 the Bureau announced a revised plan for achieving the needed quality in the MAF-TIGER. The new plan called for expanded field canvassing operations in 1998 and 1999 in a manner similar to the traditional, blanket canvassing operations used in prior censuses. This effort was to be in combination with an opportunity for local governments to review the Bureau's address list under the Local Update of Census Addresses (LUCA) program. The addition of expanded USPS operations (e.g., casing checks to update the address list after the census canvassing and LUCA operations) will then provide the final updates to MAF-TIGER just prior to mailout of the census questionnaires.

---

[1]The urban canvassing was aimed largely at multi-unit structures and areas with conversions from single to multi-unit structures.

A dual canvassing strategy has been and is now being implemented in 1998 and 1999, making a distinction between areas that are largely urban with mail delivery based on city-style addresses and areas that are largely rural (which may or may not have city-style addresses), where USPS delivery is generally not based on a city-style address. For largely urban areas, the Bureau assumed that the existing MAF-TIGER was of sufficiently high quality to enable local governments to review the current address list, that is, to initiate the LUCA program, starting in the summer of 1998. Following the receipt of LUCA feedback from local governments, the Bureau will conduct a full field canvass of all urban blocks in 1999. The canvass will deal with all LUCA challenges, will check every third address in each block, and will check all addresses in multi-unit structures and structures where conversions from single to multi-unit status were occurring. For largely rural areas, the Bureau planned to conduct a full field canvass of housing units (listing all addresses and noting the location of housing units on census maps), starting no later than fall 1998. The resulting updates to the MAF-TIGER for rural areas will be distributed by spring 1999 to local governments for review under the LUCA program.

The ability to carry out the above operations with little error depends on (1) the recruitment and supervision of a high quality field staff to carry out the expanded field canvassing operations in the limited time available, (2) the technical ability to manage the field data and its proper entry into the MAF-TIGER files, and (3) the ability to partner work with local governments to make the most of the local review of addresses and the resulting incorporation of verifiable corrections into the MAF-TIGER files.

There is no time in the schedule of events leading up to the 2000 census to alter current plans concerning MAF-TIGER improvements. Given the Bureau's recognition of the uneven quality of the decade-long efforts to keep the MAF-TIGER up to date, it has returned to intensive field operations as the best way to achieve the level of uniformity, accuracy, and completeness needed to conduct the census enumeration as planned. The dependence of this strategy on securing the people and technical resources needed to make it succeed entails a risk: while the canvassing procedures to be used are not new, mounting a far larger and more expensive field effort than was originally planned and implementing it successfully in the time that remains may be difficult.

Some important implications of the new MAF-TIGER improvement plan with respect to the issues, concerns, and recommendations presented in the panel's second interim report are discussed below.

MAF-TIGER Updating—Urban Areas

The strategy of having LUCA precede the full-block canvassing is based on the desire to give local governments the best opportunity to participate in LUCA and to hold off on field canvassing until a date closer to the actual census. While this may be the best operational way to proceed, it does present some concerns. First, it assumes that the acknowledged limitations of the procedures used so far to keep MAF-TIGER up to date were not extensive so that it is worthwhile for local governments to review the existing list before field canvassing. The MAF-TIGER is not likely to be as accurate and up to date as desirable. This is particularly true with regard to multi-unit addresses. These limitations need to be clearly communicated to and understood by local governments reviewing these lists.

Second, even under this plan, local governments participating in LUCA will only have 3 months to review the MAF-TIGER. This, coupled with limited local resources and capacity for systematically reviewing the Census Bureau's list, may result in targeted local review of areas that are thought to be especially incorrect or incomplete. This targeting may result in some address list deficiencies that remain undiscovered.

Third, the format in which MAF-TIGER files are provided for local government review and the requirements for how local officials report challenges to the address list may limit local participation in the review process. Only 34 of 60 jurisdictions participated in LUCA in the 1998 census dress rehearsal (U.S. General Accounting Office, 1998).

Finally, the Census Bureau must incorporate the local challenges under LUCA into its field canvassing operations and then provide feedback to local governments on their challenges. It is extremely important that local governments are assured that the needed MAF-TIGER quality has been achieved in order to garner their support for the enumeration operations that follow.

LUCA Program

The Census Bureau is soliciting participation in the LUCA program by sending letters of invitation to the highest elected officials of all units of local government. The response to this program, even with intensive Bureau telephone follow-up, may well be uneven in terms of the geography and population covered by participating governments. Those who elect to participate are invited to local LUCA training workshops (multiple sites in each state): the workshops were conducted in the spring of 1998 for jurisdictions with urban areas, and workshops for rural areas were planned for early 1999. These steps are necessary, but they may not suffice to ensure a significant impact of the LUCA program on the final quality of the MAF-TIGER. As noted in the panel's second interim report (National Research Council, 1997b), the effectiveness of the LUCA program depends on the rate of participation by local governments, the extent and quality of the changes they propose, and the Census Bureau's ability to incorporate the needed changes and corrections and convey them back to the local governments.

Ultimately, the quality of the expanded canvassing operations in both urban and rural areas will determine the major quality improvements to the MAF-TIGER. The LUCA program will be a contributor, although its impact may be as much one of perception as of making improvements to MAF-TIGER.

Multi-Unit Structures

The panel's observations in its second interim report regarding multi-unit structures remain relevant. The panel suggested that LUCA pay special attention to structures that have units either without clear or unique labels or units that are not clearly distinguishable. The panel also suggested that it might even be preferable in some cases to treat an entire structure as the "dwelling unit" for purposes of the MAF, nonresponse follow-up, and integrated coverage measurement (ICM). At this time, this idea should be seen as only a possibility for 2010, since it will create complications with respect to the sample design for nonresponse follow-up and for ICM matching rules, but it should be considered for 2010. Clearly, the expanded canvassing operations must address the problem of enumerating households in multi-unit structures. It is likely that many of the LUCA challenges from local government will involve multi-unit structures. This is where the current MAF-TIGER is likely to be weakest, in the absence of prior field canvassing before LUCA review in the urban areas. If the current MAF-TIGER is weak for multi-unit structures, this contributes to the risk that is taken in having local governments review the MAF-TIGER before final field canvassing.

The revised Census Bureau plan, with its emphasis on a full precensus field check, removes from the Bureau the burden of predicting where its current files are inaccurate and then performing only targeted field checks to achieve the required level of quality. Instead, the Bureau is substituting a proven procedure, albeit one that is more expensive, which requires a large field implementation to succeed and that makes certain assumptions about the ability of urban areas to participate in LUCA before this field canvass will take place.

Recommendation 3.1: The panel endorses the Census Bureau's plan to conduct a full canvass of the areas covered by the MAF-TIGER, which began in the fall of 1998 and will continue through 1999. In addition, the panel recommends that the Bureau investigate the usefulness of other data sources for updating MAF-TIGER during the coming decade, including address lists and maps from private companies and residential housing data from property tax records and maps.

DATE OF CENSUS DAY

In preparing for the 2000 census the Census Bureau considered pursuing legislation to move the date of the census from April 1 to mid-March (while retaining the mandated delivery dates of state counts by December 31 and counts for redistricting by the following April 1). The panel regrets that this change was not pursued. The proposed date change would have had two major advantages: (1) a likely improvement in the quality of coverage and (2) some additional time to complete critical coverage studies, data processing, and analysis of results prior to the December 31 deadline for releasing state counts.

Improvement in the quality of coverage would result from moving the census date away from the end of the month, when changes of address are most common. The concentration of moves at the time of the census leads to both a greater likelihood of households failing to complete and return a questionnaire and increased chances of duplicate reporting. Such reporting problems increase the volume and complexity of the workload associated with both nonresponse follow-up and coverage measurement efforts. A reduction in these workloads would result in both improved data quality and reduced costs. While the extent of improvements in the quality of coverage or reductions in costs is difficult to estimate, experience with the most recent census of Canada suggests that the benefits would be significant. Statistics Canada has not estimated the exact benefits, but agency officials attribute both lower undercoverage and reduced costs to a change in the 1996 census date from the beginning of June to mid-May.

The two weeks or more of additional time that would be gained by moving census day from April 1 to mid-March would benefit census operations. Current schedules for completing the census data collection, post-enumeration coverage data collection, data processing, and review of results are extremely tight. There is little time to resolve unforeseen problems or to extend schedules where workloads have been underestimated. The added time could reduce the likelihood of errors of commission or omission, and improve data quality by extended nonresponse follow-up, more thorough coverage studies, and more extensive quality checks.

Recommendation 3.2: The panel recommends that Congress enact legislation to move the date of the 2010 census to mid-March.

The panel is concerned that the Census Bureau has attempted to accommodate the failure to move the census day to earlier than April 1 by mailing out census questionnaires earlier. However, this does not gain as much time as might be thought since residents are not required to return the questionnaire until census day and it is not likely to lessen the difficulties posed by movers at the end of the month. Depending on how much earlier questionnaires are mailed, it could also exacerbate data quality and coverage problems since many people may complete and return their questionnaire well in advance of census day. This would increase the number of changes caused by moves, births, and deaths, which would have to be revised in coverage measurement studies and, with the use of a blanket second mailout, would likely increase the degree of multiple responses. Finally, it makes the census reference date somewhat ambiguous and may increase the number of situations in which people who move and are in the integrated coverage measurement survey have a different residence for April 1 or later but had a March residence for the census.

USE OF MULTIPLE RESPONSE OPPORTUNITIES

For the past few censuses there have been complaints from individuals who thought either that their residence had been left off the census mailing list or that they had been omitted from the questionnaire returned for their household of residence. While the great majority of these complaints proved not to be true, the "Were You Counted?" programs of the 1980 and 1990 censuses provided an opportunity for those who believed they were missed to be included and thus were a useful public relations tool.

The public relations value of the 2000 census analog, the "Be Counted" program, is therefore incontestable. "Be Counted" provides an easy way for residents who do not receive (or believe they did not receive) a census form or believe they were otherwise not counted to return a census questionnaire (available in various public locations) or to telephone in their response. This easy access reduces respondent burden and could target historically undercounted groups. This program was adopted from a suggestion presented to Congress by the U.S. General Accounting Office (1992). The forms are available in foreign languages, and individuals can request by telephone a census form in a large number of languages. A key difference between the "Were You Counted?" and "Be Counted" programs is that the first was concurrent with nonresponse follow-up, and the latter is concurrent with the mailout/mailback portion of the census.

One area worthy of more research is that of assessing the extent to which additional people are whole-household versus within-household additions and whether the households are included on the MAF. For whole-household additions that are from addresses on the MAF, this program would simply reduce the nonresponse follow-up workload. For whole-household additions not on the MAF and additions to MAF households that were partially enumerated, this program would reduce undercoverage. In the 1998 dress rehearsal, nonresponse follow-up was conducted on those forms that indicated that responses were for a partial household (and for "Be Counted" forms that were received late from MAF addresses). In addition, it might be useful to conduct field follow-up of some whole-household additions for addresses both on and not on the MAF. For addresses not on the MAF, this would be helpful in understanding how the MAF was deficient and in verifying additional households. For addresses on the MAF, this would be useful in determining whether the response of whole-household additions was accurate.

Another area worth examining is whether respondents should continue to be required to report on the census form whether their response is for a whole or a partial household. The response to this question currently determines whether the household is included in nonresponse follow-up. There is evidence to suggest that this information may be inaccurate. Therefore, as mentioned above, the validity of this information should be examined.

Along with the public relations and modest enumeration benefits, the "Be Counted" program raises one primary concern, which is that there is a potential to have many households in the 2000 census for which more than one questionnaire is returned (representing either the same household or a partial household).[2] The frequency of this duplication in the 1995 test census was not excessive enough (15 percent of the responses were for individuals who were already enumerated) to produce an unfeasible amount of "unduplication." However, it might be a far greater problem in the 2000 census, because of either increased amounts of undiscovered unduplication or a more compressed time schedule, making unduplication either much more time consuming or error prone. Therefore, the results from the 1998 census dress rehearsal in evaluating the primary selection algorithm, which determines which forms are considered to be duplicates, should be used to better understand the problems

---

[2]Another concern is the number of fictitious or incorrect enumerations that are received.

that this program will raise and to assess modifications that will make it more effective.

USE OF BLANKET REPLACEMENT QUESTIONNAIRES

The panel has been enthusiastic about targeted mailing of replacement questionnaires to reduce nonresponse (see National Research Council, 1997a). Testing in a variety of situations indicated that this could have been one of the most important innovations in the 2000 census. Unfortunately, the size and time constraints of the 2000 census seem to require that replacement questionnaires be mailed to all census addresses, not only the nonresponding ones.

While there is still likely to be a substantial increase in response among mail nonrespondents with a blanket mailing of replacement questionnaires, the panel foresees the potential for large numbers of duplicate responses. In addition, if what is being done is not well understood by the public, there is a possibility of a public relations problem if people feel unnecessarily bothered by the Census Bureau after responding promptly to the first questionnaire they received. Furthermore, the cost and environmental impact of a blanket second mailing are likely to elicit some negative comments from the public. Clearly, more analysis and experience with this technique are needed before firm recommendations can be given. It would be useful to have a direct analysis of the costs and benefits of the use of a blanket second mailing of questionnaires sometime early in the next planning cycle. The 1998 dress rehearsal will provide some important evidence as to the value of blanket replacement questionnaires, and final decisions about their use in the 2000 census should not be made until the dress rehearsal experience is evaluated. In addition, the Census Bureau should determine early in the next decade whether it will be technologically feasible to use a targeted replacement questionnaire in the 2010 census, since that is the strongly preferred procedure.

> **Recommendation 3.3: If the 1998 census dress rehearsal gives any indication that there are substantial problems (of extensive duplication of returned forms or public dissatisfaction) associated with the use of a blanket replacement form mailing, this procedure should be dropped and only a reminder postcard sent to each household. Furthermore, the Census Bureau should explore all possible approaches to having available, for the 2010 census, technology that will permit targeted mailing of second forms only to households that did not return their first forms by a specific date.**

LONG-FORM SAMPLING RATES

The Census Bureau will use four long-form sampling rates for governmental units[3] in the 2000 census (and used them in the 1998 census dress rehearsal): 1 in 2, 1 in 4, 1 in 6, and 1 in 8, depending on the number of housing units in a jurisdiction. This represents a change from the 1990 census—the addition of a fourth intermediate step, the 1-in-4 sampling rate. The panel endorses this and related decisions affecting the design of long-form sampling for the 2000 census.

The Census Bureau is making one other change of note with respect to the assignment of long-form sampling rates: the sampling rate cutoffs will be based solely on the counts of addresses or housing units. In contrast, in 1990 the Bureau used a combination of population and housing unit counts to define the size of units for purposes of sampling. With these changes, the geographical units to which the long-form sampling will be applied will be configured somewhat differently than if the 1990 design were being used in 2000. The addition of a fourth sampling rate provides the Bureau with greater flexibility in achieving the goal of an overall long-form sampling rate of approximately 17 percent (1 in 6) of all addresses nationally—the same as in 1990—with more nearly equal precision for small areas. The fourth rate will reduce the disparity in coefficients of variation between areas of similar size that would have fallen on opposite sides of a threshold and as a result be sampled at 1-in-2 and 1-in-6 rates, respectively. The change might also help ease the transition from the census long form to the American Community Survey,[4] which will also use four sampling rates.

The 1-in-2 rate will be applied to governmental units (including school districts) with fewer than 800 housing units, while the new 1-in-4 rate will be applied to governmental units with 800 to 1,200 housing units. Governmental units that exceed this size will have sampling rates set by census tract. The 1-in-6 rate will be applied to census tracts with fewer than 2,000 housing units (that do not satisfy the above conditions for higher sampling rates), while the minimum 1-in-8 rate will be applied to census tracts of 2,000 or more housing units. These cutoffs were selected from simulation studies that considered a variety of factors affecting the overall response rate and the resulting coefficients of variation. With the addition of a fourth sampling rate, some units will be sampled at a lower

---

[3]A governmental unit is a county, town, township, specified unincorporated area, school district, etc.

[4]The American Community Survey is a proposed mailout/mailback survey of 3 million households annually using a so-called rolling sample design. The content will be similar to that of the decennial census long form.

rate than would otherwise have been the case (1 in 4 instead of 1 in 2). The panel agrees with the Census Bureau that the likely increase in the coefficient of variation for these areas is more than offset by the reduction in variances for areas that are sampled at the 1-in-4 instead of the 1-in-6 rate and the narrowing of differences in reliability across areas generally. Nevertheless, if the long form is used in the 2010 census, the panel encourages a further look at strategies to reduce differences in coefficients of variation among areas that are sampled at rates above the minimum.

Recommendation 3.4: The panel supports the addition of a fourth sampling rate for the collection of long-form data in the 2000 census and encourages further research to reduce differences in coefficients of variation among areas if the long form is used in the 2010 census.

SAMPLING RATE FOR VACANT UNITS

During the 1995 census test, 6 percent of prenotice letters and 7 percent of initial questionnaires across the two urban sites were returned by postmasters as "undeliverable as addressed" (UAA). About two-thirds of such returns identified the units as vacant rather than nonvacant (e.g., nonexistent or bad address). It is not clear to the panel how to handle the nonvacant UAA postmaster returns, so they are not further discussed. In 1990 all postmaster returns of the census form (there was no prenotice letter) were visited by enumerators to verify whether the units were vacant or nonexistent. Early plans for the 2000 census called for follow-up visits to a 1-in-10 sample of postmaster returns identified as vacant and estimation for the other 90 percent, in an operation separate from the main nonresponse follow-up. In census tests in Oakland, California, and Paterson, New Jersey, 66 and 59 percent, respectively, of households initially identified as vacant were in fact discovered to be vacant, so it makes sense to handle vacant units from postmaster returns separately from the main nonresponse follow-up to reduce the time between census day and follow-up operations and, in the event of a targeted replacement questionnaire, to avoid the cost of mailing replacement questionnaires.

In its second interim report (National Research Council, 1997b) the panel argued that the 10 percent sampling rate was not optimal since, assuming equal costs, the ratio of sampling rates for two strata should be proportional to the ratio of the within-strata standard deviations. Given that the overall nonresponse follow-up sampling rate is about 70 percent,[5] a 10 percent follow-up rate for postmaster returns identified as

---

[5]With an overall mail response rate of 65 percent, getting to 90 percent as a result of nonresponse follow-up will require sampling 25 of the remaining 35 percent, or a sampling rate of 71 percent.

vacant would be too low unless those cases were considerably less variable. The panel has undertaken some preliminary calculations based on the assumption that the household distribution for nonvacant (initially designated vacant) UAA units is the same as that for nonvacant households with deliverable addresses. These calculations indicate that the sampling variances are close. With an occupation rate of about 30 percent, the variance of household counts for units identified as vacant by postmaster returns should be roughly the same as that for the main nonresponse follow-up sample, arguing for a sampling rate closer to that for nonresponse follow-up.[6] The panel therefore recommended that optimal design theory guide the choice of higher sampling rates for units that postmasters identified as vacant. While optimal design theory would seemingly support a higher UAA-vacant sampling rate than the selected one of 30 percent, since the overall sampling rate for nonresponse follow-up is expected to be roughly 70 percent, it is important to keep in mind that the sampling rate for nonresponse follow-up was not determined solely through optimal design considerations. The variance reduction in moving from 10 to 30 percent is much more important to achieve than the benefit from moving from 30 to 70 percent.

The Census Bureau has since undertaken a cost-effectiveness analysis of the sampling rate for UAA vacants by comparing the varying costs and coefficients of variation obtained from various sampling rates. This analysis is consistent with a sampling rate of 30 percent. The panel supports this change in strategy, noting that this new recommended sampling rate of 30 percent for UAA vacants is close to that for nonresponse follow-up for high-response areas (1 in 3), relating back to the argument from optimal design theory. Since the fraction of the workload that is represented by UAA vacants is relatively small, except where there is very high mailback response, sampling at the rate of nonresponse follow-up for high mailback areas seems appropriate, especially if, as assumed, the interviews have about the same cost and the variance ratios are close to 1.

---

[6]The detailed argument is as follows: The variance of the household counts for units identified as vacant, assuming that the distribution of the nonvacant UAA households is the same as that for the nonvacant nonresponse follow-up cases (with mean μ and variance σ^2), is $.3\sigma^2 + .7(.3)\mu^2$. This exceeds σ^2 when the coefficient of variation is less than .55 among the nonresponse follow-up cases, which is likely; hence, one should act as if the optimal rate for UAA vacants is at least as high as for nonresponse follow-up. In a 1995 census test file for occupied units, μ was 2.5 and σ was 1.6. Based on these values, for occupancy rates of .2, .3, and .4, the standard deviations are 1.22, 1.43, and 1.57, respectively. Of course, some of the nonresponse follow-ups are also vacant, but occupancy rates above .8 yield standard deviations around 1.6. Therefore, the UAA sampling rate should be approximately the same as the average nonresponse follow-up rate. A complication is that these calculations might be considerably different for subareas.

There is reason to believe that UAA vacant interviews may be slightly less expensive than nonresponse follow-up interviews since such interviews are conducted outside the peak load time for nonresponse follow-up. This would suggest an even higher sampling rate.

> **Recommendation 3.5: The panel supports the Census Bureau's decision to increase the sampling rate for units identified as vacant by the U.S. Postal Service to a rate greater than 1 in 10, as originally proposed. The current proposed sampling rate of 3 in 10 is therefore preferred.**

USE OF NONRESPONSE FOLLOW-UP TO DIRECTLY ENUMERATE AT LEAST 90 PERCENT OF HOUSEHOLDS

In 1990 the Census Bureau conducted nonresponse follow-up of all housing units that failed to respond by mail to the census questionnaire. This process, which required field enumerators to visit housing units one or more times, cost an estimated $1.4 billion (National Research Council, 1995). In the 2000 census the Census Bureau plans to sample, for nonresponse field follow-up, housing units that have not responded by mail or other means within 6 weeks of mailout of the first questionnaire. In each census tract with a (presampling) response rate of less than 85 percent, the Bureau will sample enough housing units to reach a final response of 90 percent for the tract. For example, if a tract's response rate is 70 percent, each nonresponding housing unit would have a two-thirds probability of being sampled for nonresponse follow-up, so two-thirds of the 30 percent of nonrespondents would be included in the sample. In tracts with presampling response rates of 85 percent or higher, the Bureau will sample one-third of housing units.

The panel endorses the decision to sample at a rate of at least 1 in 3 for all tracts, even where that will raise the final response rate above 90 percent. Doing so will avoid undesirably large sampling errors in high-response tracts (see National Research Council, 1997b). However, the panel notes that considerable variation in the size of standard errors will remain across equal-sized tracts with different initial response rates. The panel believes that a very desirable property of a sample design for nonresponse follow-up is that the sampling error should not be a function of the initial response rate (except in the limit). In addition, given the multitude of uses of census numbers, an argument can be made that an equal coefficient of variation design at the tract level is consistent with the collection of census counts with good properties across a wide variety of applications. Relaxing the requirement to achieve a 90 percent response rate in all tracts would allow a design specification that achieves near equity in coefficients of variation across regions regardless of initial response rate.[7] The panel believes that the Census Bureau should evaluate alternative design specifications of this type for 2010.

Finally, another possible drawback to the current plan for 2000 is that, nationally, a higher proportion of initial nonrespondent households will be visited (roughly three-quarters) than would ordinarily be from the perspective of quality and cost per additional sampled unit. The high sampling rate for nonresponse follow-up limits opportunities for cost savings and quality improvement as a result of finishing follow-up earlier. Because this is the first time that sampling for nonresponse follow-up is being planned for the decennial census, however, there are clearly virtues in proceeding conservatively. In addition, because of the myriad uses and users of census information, the tradeoff of variance and cost is different for various users, which is another reason to proceed conservatively. The present plan ensures low coefficients of variation from the use of sampling for nonresponse follow-up for relatively small units of census geography. The panel understands and endorses the Census Bureau's desire to use a plan with this property, even at the expense of retaining a relatively high overall rate of nonresponse follow-up with the associated limits on cost savings and quality improvements.[8]

Recommendation 3.6: The Census Bureau should explore the advantages of sample designs for nonresponse follow-up that do not require a predetermined response rate and that can therefore achieve near equity in coefficients of variation across region, regardless of initial response rates.

HOT DECK IMPUTATION FOR NONRESPONSE FOLLOW-UP AND UAA VACANT HOUSEHOLDS

For the 2000 census the plan is to use sampling for both nonresponse follow-up and UAA units initially identified as vacant households. The information from the sampled (mail) nonrespondents is used to provide estimates for those that were not sampled, resulting in estimated counts

---

[7]For specifics on the possible gains of an equal coefficient of variation design, see National Research Council (1997b:Table 1).

[8]The Census Bureau includes all UAA vacants as responses in its assessment of achieving a response rate of 90 percent in each tract. This will generally make little difference, and it is not entirely clear how UAA vacants should be included since many are occupied. However, it would probably be preferable not to include UAA vacants in this assessment since that conforms better with the general perception of what "percentage responding" implies.

for a given tract. A variety of procedures for doing this can be considered: (1) duplicating each sampled respondent's data an integral number of times equal (or approximately equal) to the sample weight for the respondent less one; (2) hot deck imputation, which is nearly identical to the first procedure, the same integral number of times; or (3) some type of model-based estimation. The leading exemplar of the second approach is sequential nearest-neighbor hot deck imputation based on the household's multi-unit status. (This status and geography are the only information available for nonrespondents.) In this process, all mail nonrespondents who are not sampled for nonresponse follow-up will have their household data imputed from a geographically close mail nonrespondent with the same multi-unit status that was selected for the nonrespondent follow-up sample. The number of times a sampled household can be used as an imputation donor is limited. (Given that the Census Bureau is committed to providing its users' with data files in which each household receives a unit weight, any procedure must be convertible to a file of households with unit weights.)

The Census Bureau conducted some initial research on this topic (see Farber, 1997), in which the first procedure and variations of the second (allowing hot deck substitutions from surrounding geographic regions of varying sizes) were compared. Variations of the third procedure, especially a model-based imputation method developed by Schafer et al. (1993), were not included in the research because of their operational demands and difficulty of communication to users.

The advantage of the third type of procedure instead of the second is that variations of the third procedure might use the data more effectively (not necessarily being restricted to two passes through the data file) in producing the imputations. Given the variety of innovations being planned for the 2000 census, there is a strong interest in keeping things as straightforward as possible, especially when the benefits of more complicated processes are relatively modest. This appears to apply in this case since the amount of information available on nonrespondents is limited. The Census Bureau has decided to use sequential nearest-neighbor hot deck imputation, the methodology that has a long history of use in the decennial census in treating various forms of nonresponse. Given its relative ease of use, its success in the past, and the fact that geographical proximity is usually a relatively strong predictor of similarity of race and housing type, it is a sensible choice. Furthermore, its scale in 2000 will be expanded relative to 1990, which may improve its performance. More research should be conducted to ascertain the impact of sequential nearest-neighbor hot deck imputation on bias and variance of the census counts, if not before the 2000 census, then during planning for the 2010 census, since methods from the third procedure above may have advantages.

Recommendation 3.7: Given the current state of technical knowledge and the time available, the panel endorses the Census Bureau's plan for sequential hot deck imputation of nonsampled nonresponding and post office-designated vacant households. Substantial research should be conducted using data from the 2000 census to develop enhanced procedures for future censuses.

Using results from the census dress rehearsal, it will be important to check if there are substantial differences between the characteristics of the mail respondents and nonrespondents. If there are not, the donor pool for the imputations should be extended to mail respondents.

USE OF COMPUTER-ASSISTED PERSONAL INTERVIEWING FOR INTEGRATED COVERAGE MEASUREMENT

The Census Bureau has decided that its integrated coverage measurement (ICM) interviewing staff will use laptop computers and computer-assisted personal interviewing (CAPI) technology in the 1998 census dress rehearsal and, pending success in that trial, in the 2000 census. This will be the first use of laptops by interviewers in a U.S. decennial census. The decision reflects the overall goal of the Bureau to make use of the latest technologies as part of the reengineered 2000 census. The plan is for interviewers to use CAPI technology not only for initial personal interviewing, but also in reinterviews conducted for quality assurance purposes and in the ICM personal follow-up interview. The additional costs over a paper-and-pencil administration of the same survey are estimated to be $60 million.

The panel supports this decision despite its increased cost because using laptops and CAPI for ICM interviewing will very likely save time at a critical stage of data collection and is also likely to improve the quality of the data. The Census Bureau estimates that interviewer use of laptops and CAPI will save 12 work days during ICM data collection, since the time required for mailing questionnaires to a data capture center for editing, scanning, and keying will be eliminated. Another likely benefit of speed in the quality assurance reinterviewing portion of ICM is that any fabrication of data by interviewers can be detected and eliminated more quickly.

The panel also believes that the data collected via CAPI are likely to be of higher quality for several reasons. First, interviewer errors in skip patterns[9] will be eliminated, and edits that are built into the instrument

---

[9]A skip pattern is a pattern of questions that a respondent is or is not asked based on the responses to previous questions on a survey form.

can alert the interviewer to resolve certain kinds of errors on the spot with help from the respondent. Also, some research suggests that interviewers prefer CAPI to paper and pencil and that it increases their perception of the importance of their job. The experience of the Census Bureau in its 1996 community census further suggested that the novelty of the CAPI interview was helpful in motivating respondents.

However, there are some risks with this decision. First, interviewers will need to be trained in a new set of skills to use CAPI, in addition to the skills required for interviewing. It is possible that job candidates with computer skills (or the aptitude to be easily trained) may be more difficult to find or more expensive to hire than candidates without those skills. It is also possible that there will be increased need for computer support personnel, who might be difficult to hire in sufficient numbers. While the panel cannot offer any suggestions in this difficult area, there is the hope that further evaluation based on the dress rehearsal experience will make clear the tradeoffs in the use of CAPI for this important data collection in 2000.

TREATMENT OF MISSING DATA IN INTEGRATED COVERAGE MEASUREMENT

Plans have been made for dealing with several types of missing data that will appear in the ICM process, with an emphasis on simplicity of methodology. Non-interview adjustment relates to occupied housing units for which no post-enumeration survey interview can be obtained:[10] the weight of these units, using a standard weighting adjustment, will be spread across interviewed units in the same block cluster and type of housing unit, similar to the procedure used in the 1990 census. The imputation of characteristics information (other than household attachment), necessary for persons whose characteristics were not obtained in the integrated coverage measurement interview, will be accomplished through the use of characteristics for the same person collected in the census, when available, or through use of information from other persons in the same or nearby households when census information is not available.

Match status, residence status,[11] and correct enumeration status are key variables for calculating adjustment factors. When these are missing, it is usually because insufficient identifying information was collected to

---

[10]The ICM non-interview rate in the 1995 census test in Oakland, California, was 5.6 percent (Gbur, 1996).

[11]Residence status is the assessment of whether someone resides at the address at which he or she is enumerated.

determine a person's status. Probabilities for these variables will be imputed using the proportions among persons whose status was resolved in the same state. This procedure is much simpler but makes less use of background information about the unresolved cases than the hierarchical logistic regression procedure used in the 1990 census. The rationale for this change is that the 1990 procedure would become more difficult to implement in 2000 because of the requirement of fitting separate models in each state, while the simplified procedure is more acceptable because operational improvements have greatly reduced the amount of missing data. If missing-data rates are shown to have been low in the 1998 census dress rehearsal, the panel considers this decision appropriate, but it should be reconsidered if missing-data rates are at the 1990 levels.

DEMOGRAPHIC ANALYSIS AND INTEGRATED COVERAGE MEASUREMENT

Given current plans, there will be two methods available to assess the amount of net undercoverage in the 2000 census—integrated coverage measurement and demographic analysis. Counts from demographic analysis have been used for several decades as an estimate of overall net undercoverage and nationally for some demographic groups. Demographic analysis requires relatively complete information on emigration and immigration, both documented and undocumented. Unfortunately, because of its dependence on information about migration which is incomplete in many respects, demographic analysis provides useful information on net undercoverage only at the national level, and then only for some demographic groups (notably, for blacks and not for Hispanics). (See National Research Council, 1994, for details of each of these methods, and Robinson et al., 1993, for an analysis of the errors in demographic analysis.) Historically, (proposed) adjustments based on dual-system estimation and post-enumeration surveys have resulted in estimated population counts for black males that are intermediate to those of the census and demographic analysis, and many analysts believe that demographic analysis provides better assessments of undercoverage nationally for black males. Given these two sources of information, the hope might be to combine them to produce a superior set of undercoverage estimates.

Bell (1993) suggests several methods for combining these two sources of information, specifically the information from dual-system estimation and the sex ratios (ratios of the number of women to the number of men within age/race groups) from demographic analysis. Bell describes several approaches that are equally plausible for using the demographic analysis information at lower levels of aggregation, which result in relatively different sets of counts. Failure to use information from demographic analysis appropriately could result in estimates (at certain levels of aggregation) that would be inferior to reasonable methods that use this information. However, it is difficult to recommend a specific alternative at this time without some empirical basis. It should also be noted that the models proposed by Bell all make use of the strong assumption that dual-system estimates are unbiased for females, which is a difficult assumption to support, and the sensitivity of Bell's methods to this assumption is unknown. Validation of assumptions and selection of a preferred method depend on further research, which the panel strongly supports. Therefore, the panel agrees with the current view of the Census Bureau not to incorporate information from demographic analysis into estimates from the 2000 census. Research should be undertaken to show how to best incorporate this source of data in future censuses.

USE OF DUAL-SYSTEM ESTIMATION

In planning for the 2000 census the Census Bureau considered two basic designs for integrated coverage measurement: a post-enumeration survey (PES) with dual-system estimation, and the Census Plus survey design and estimation methodology. The key features of these designs are discussed in previous reports of this panel and its predecessor (National Research Council, 1994, 1997b), and are briefly summarized here.

The PES is a survey conducted after, and independently of, the initial census enumeration (mailback and nonresponse follow-up) in a sample of blocks or block clusters, using an independently created list of housing units. Residents of a housing unit are asked who lived there on census day, using an interview with special probes designed to elicit as complete a roster of household members as possible. The results of this interview are matched against the original roster collected by mail or nonresponse follow-up return (in the PES sample blocks, nonresponse follow-up is carried out for 100 percent of nonrespondents), and discrepancies are resolved, using follow-up interviews if necessary, to determine whether each person was or was not actually a census day resident. Using the survey results, two ratios are calculated: (1) the fraction of census day residents found in the PES who were missed by the initial enumeration (omissions) and (2) the fraction of people in the initial enumeration who should not have been counted at or near that address (erroneous enumerations). Under the assumption that omission rates in the initial enumeration are the same for people who are not found in the PES as for those who are, it is possible to estimate an adjustment factor—that is, the number by which the count in the initial enumeration must be multiplied in order to estimate the actual number of residents. The dual-system estimation method gets its name from the fact that data from two independent data-collection systems, the initial enumeration and the PES, are combined to obtain the required factors. (The precise formula for dual-system estimation is provided in Chapter 2.)

As in the PES, in the Census Plus coverage measurement survey interviewers go to a sample of housing units and first ask the residents who lived there on census day. Census Plus adds a second phase to the interview in which the interviewer attempts to reconcile the roster from the first phase of the interview with the initial census enumeration that has been loaded into the interviewer's laptop computer, to obtain a "resolved roster." Little or no follow-up is conducted after this two-phase interview. For estimation purposes the resolved roster is regarded as the truth, so the adjustment factor is essentially the ratio of the count in the resolved roster to the count in the initial enumeration.

Because Census Plus treats the resolved roster as final, the quality of its estimated adjustment factors is critically dependent on the completeness of that roster. Dual-system estimation, on the other hand, requires that the PES be statistically independent of the initial enumeration but not necessarily complete. It also requires a matching operation. Even if the independence assumption is not entirely correct (because people in various poststrata who are missed by the PES are also more likely than others to be omitted from the initial enumeration), dual-system estimation will usually be intermediate to the census and the true counts. (This argument is developed more fully in Chapter 4.) The completeness of the final roster was listed as an essential requirement for use of the Census Plus methodology in 2000 (see National Research Council, 1994, especially, Recommendation 4.3). In the 1995 test census, however, the Census Plus resolved rosters omitted many residents. Although this was due in part to processing delays in the test, which caused many interviews to be conducted without an initial enumeration roster for use in reconciliation, the 1995 experience suggests that the problems with undercoverage by Census Plus are unlikely to be overcome before 2000. The panel's independent analysis of the test evaluations (National Research Council, 1997b) pointed in this direction, and the panel supports the decision of the Census Bureau not to use Census Plus in the 2000 census.

The PES methodology has been used before, notably in the 1990 census, in a form similar to that planned for the 2000 census, although the resulting counts were not used for apportionment or redistricting in 1990. The primary difficulty with the PES for 2000 concerns scheduling because of the additional follow-up operations that are required. A decennial census schedule that allows time for the PES is very tight, and the panel looks forward to the results of efforts by the Census Bureau to accelerate the PES by allowing it to partially overlap the initial enumeration time schedule.

The PES also must be adapted to be used jointly with nonresponse follow-up sampling. This is an important issue for people who move between census day and the PES enumeration. In 1990 the PES sample consisted of people resident in sample blocks at the time of the PES survey ("PES-B"), but in the 2000 census some of those people will have moved in from other blocks where only a sample of the households were included in nonresponse follow-up. Therefore, under the PES-B design, it is sometimes not just difficult (as in 1990), but impossible to determine who would have been included in the original enumeration if they had not responded by mail and not been sampled in nonresponse follow-up. For this reason, procedures for the 1995 and 1996 test censuses defined the PES sample as consisting of people resident in PES sample housing units on census day ("PES-A"); when a household moves shortly after census day, the PES requires finding and interviewing the family that moved out. The Census Bureau's plan for the 1998 census dress rehearsal called for use of a hybrid, third method ("PES-C") in which the match rate is estimated either through the use of proxy information collected from the people moving in or at times by reinterviewing the family that moved out, but the number of people in "mover" households (where "mover" means the broad population of households that move at this time) is estimated from the residents found in the PES. It is thought that this estimated number is superior to that obtained from outmovers (for details, see Bureau of the Census, 1997). The panel believes that the mover problem can be solved, and it urges the Census Bureau to act more quickly to develop and test methodology for the treatment of movers. (The problem may be reduced through more expedited nonresponse follow-up.)

BORROWING INFORMATION ACROSS STATES

One of the arguments against adjusting the 1990 census was that the empirical Bayes regression smoothing, which was used to borrow information across the 1,392 (original) poststrata, used information from other states to produce estimated counts for a given state. The empirical Bayes regression was needed for the following reason. The use of nearly 1,400 poststrata, defined using demographic characteristics, owner/renter, and geography, produced aggregate information on census undercoverage that had generally reduced bias compared with aggregates using fewer poststrata. However, the resulting estimates had relatively high variances. To reduce these variances, smoothing across poststrata was conducted. Using some assumptions (e.g., that undercoverage for, say, black men aged 18 to 40 in metropolitan areas in Louisiana is apt to be very similar to undercoverage for black men ages 18 to 40 in metropolitan areas in South Carolina, and that shifting from one age group to another should have similar effects on undercoverage across poststrata), information from different poststrata was used to reduce the variance of the estimated undercoverage for a given stratum, possibly without appreciably increasing the bias. Smoothing or blending information from similar or easily related situations, known as "borrowing strength," can produce estimates with less overall error. Methods such as empirical and hierarchical Bayes regression modeling and closely related variance component estimates have been shown to have very desirable properties in a variety of applications (see, e.g., Gelman et al., 1995).

The need for smoothing could have been reduced had the 1990 PES been as large as initially planned. It was originally planned to have 300,000 housing units, a sample size chosen so that most direct state estimates would have been of marginally acceptable precision, though substate estimates would still have had considerable variability. However, the ultimate sample size was only about 160,000 housing units, which necessitated borrowing of information across states to obtain state-level estimates of marginally acceptable precision. Given the 750,000 housing unit PES currently planned for the 2000 census, which will permit useful estimates at lower geographic levels than the planned PES in 1990, there should be less need for smoothing.

Undercoverage of individuals in the United States is geographically determined to some extent (e.g., undercoverage is related to whether an area is urban, suburban, or rural). (Hengartner and Speed, 1993, examine the extent to which undercoverage is geographically based.) Factors other than geography also strongly affect census undercoverage. For example, the likelihood of undercoverage is higher for people whose residence is in a multi-unit structure than for those whose residence is a detached house, a factor that can vary within a single city block. It seems plausible to expect that undercoverage is similar for individuals in areas with otherwise similar characteristics that fall into states in the same region that are also generally similar. (However, there are at least two exceptions that are discussed below.) Therefore, aggregating information on census undercoverage across states is likely to improve estimated counts by reducing variance and not substantially increasing bias.

Although there are clear technical benefits from this blending of information, there is an important political concern that the responses of people outside a state could affect another state's estimated count and hence its congressional apportionment. (The advantages from a public acceptance standpoint of constraining each state's estimated counts to derive directly from information collected in that state are discussed by Fay and Thompson, 1993.) In addition, there are some difficulties in explaining these methods to nonexperts, and the ease of communication of methods for such an important purpose has its advantages. Finally, it is possible that some state effects may not be negligible—that is, areas in one state may have coverage rates that differ from those in similar areas in nearby states. An example could be when one state's census offices are more effectively run than another's, due to local economic conditions. Another example might be when the political climate in one state results in substantially different refusal rates.

A same-state constraint was not adhered to in the 1970 census. In that census the vacant/delete check was carried out on a sample basis, and state estimates used information on the residency status of "vacant" dwellings from other states. In the case of fund allocation, the distribution of Title I funds (under the Elementary and Secondary Education Act) is based on estimates of the number of poor children in counties, and regression models that blend information across counties and states are used to allocate considerable amounts of federal funds to counties and states (for a description of the method, see National Research Council, 1998). Also, with the use of sequential hot deck imputation, it is clear that at some small level of geography, the analogue of the same-state constraint is not adhered to. So, the principal rule that an area's political and monetary allocations are to be derived from information collected only from that area has not been consistently applied in past censuses or for important fund allocation programs. Also, as is relatively clear from the Title I fund allocation example, it is not even a principle that should be adhered to in all circumstances. Any use of demographic analysis, such as the promising methods examined by Bell (1993), would fail to meet the same-state principle.

The same-state constraint has strong sample design implications in that the need for direct state estimates of some threshold accuracy implies less accuracy for substate areas in large states, which has implications for the accuracy of counts of demographic groups. Furthermore, this constraint would dramatically reduce the demographic detail that could be used in the poststrata, which would result in greater heterogeneity in poststrata with respect to census undercoverage. Given the planned size of the PES (750,000 housing units), the Census Bureau is limited to about 1,000 or fewer poststrata, based on the 1990 experience. Given state-level estimates, this would mean 20 or fewer poststrata per state. One could argue that undercoverage differs substantially with respect to age, sex, race/ethnicity, and owner/renter status, possibly requiring as many as five age categories, two sex categories, three or more race/ethnicity categories, and an owner/renter dichotomous category, which results in much more then 20 poststrata in a state. As a result, a good deal of collapsing of poststrata will be required. (The Census Bureau is examining the use of "raking" to counts from aggregate poststrata to enable the use of more factors. See below for a discussion.) Of course, if state-level effects are substantial, this collapsing would be justified. However, if state-level effects are small, this collapsing will result in poststrata that join people with relatively more heterogeneous rates of census undercoverage.

Given the constraint that each state's counts be based on information collected only from that state, it is still possible to share information for substate allocation of population, as well as for congressional redistricting, when there is evidence of common patterns across groups of states. In 1990, information was used across states to produce both state counts and substate shares. Given that distributing counts within states does not violate the above constraint, its use should be considered separately.

First, consider restricting a state's estimated total count to be based only on information collected from individuals in that state. There are certainly real advantages to this restriction. It could reduce or eliminate a source of bias as discussed above—for example, if Maine's undercount is systematically greater than Vermont's within the same poststrata (groups defined by demographic characteristics, owners/renters, etc). Maine's estimated count could be lower than it should and would be if this constraint were not observed. Also, given the highly political role of state counts, not blending information is easy to understand and has great face validity. Furthermore, it could be required on legal grounds given its mention in a previous case before the Supreme Court (94-1614, 94-1631, and 94-1985; March 20, 1996).

Yet the associated cost of observing this constraint could be substantial. As mentioned above, this restriction makes inefficient use of the information collected, so that sampling error is larger than it would be through efficient use of information across states. As the National Research Council (1994:125-126) notes:

> At one extreme, a criterion of equal coefficient of variation of direct population estimates in every state (equal standard error of estimated ICM adjustment factors) would imply roughly equal sample sizes in every state, despite the 100-fold ratio of populations between the most and least populous states. Such a design might be drastically inefficient for estimation of adjustment factors for domains other than states. At the other extreme, a criterion of equal variance of direct population estimates for every state would imply larger sampling rates (and therefore disproportionately larger sample sizes) in larger states.

In order that all state estimates have a small coefficient of variation, the prohibition of not borrowing information requires that the PES sample be concentrated in small states, thereby increasing the variance of estimated counts for larger states. Also, observing this constraint does not permit, for the smallest states, substate estimation with low coefficients of variation at any level of detail.

The panel recognizes the reason for this decision, understanding that it is based on legal and political factors that are beyond the expertise and scope of a technical panel. However, there is no reason to exclude this procedure in all future censuses. A key issue is the extent to which undercoverage is related to state effects. Research on this issue would be very important to help understand the advantages obtained from observing this constraint, looking toward 2010.

The second form of this constraint is restricting the allocation of state population shares to substate areas based only on information from that state. Similar to the argument above, assuming there are consistent patterns to substate variation in adjustment factors, accepting this constraint increases the sampling variance for estimates of substate population shares. Models that allocate substate shares need to be considered separately from the methods used to estimate state population counts because substate estimates can always be controlled to add up to a given state estimate.

Two final points are important to mention. First, besides congressional apportionment, census counts are used for official purposes at various levels of aggregation, some relatively low. The constraint that an estimate be determined only using data from its geographic region is a constraint that, when viewed in its absolute form, could be extended to assert that the estimates at any level of geographic aggregation should be constructed from information collected directly from those areas. At some level of aggregation this has not been true of any modern census, is clearly unnecessarily restrictive, and therefore should not be instituted. Second, since congressional apportionment involves allocating a fixed pie of 435 representatives to the 50 states, every state's estimated count, directly estimated or not, affects every other state's apportionment.

Recommendation 3.8: The panel supports the decision of the Census Bureau to produce state total estimates using the 2000 census that are derived only from data collected within a given state. For the 2000 census, models across states should be examined for use in allocating populations within states. Both forms of the constraint on estimates that are based solely on data from a given state should be reexamined with respect to the 2010 census.

THE USE OF RAKING

The PES in the 2000 census is designed to support direct estimation for each state—that is, calculation of population estimates based only on data from a given state. PES samples will not be large enough, however, to support high-quality direct estimates for many important substate areas, such as counties, cities, and congressional districts. To generate estimates for those areas, the Census Bureau has decided to use synthetic estimation (see below), possibly combined with raking (iterative fitting of tables of counts to marginal totals).

Synthetic estimation (see Cohen, 1989) is a method of distributing estimated additional counts over those from the initial enumeration to small areas. Suppose that adjustment factors have been estimated for each of several population groups making up the population of some relatively large area, such as poststrata defined by race, age, and tenure (owner/renter) in a section of a state. The synthetic estimate of population within a poststratum for a smaller area, even a single census tract or block,[12] is obtained by applying the same adjustment factor to all people in the smaller area from the poststratum. Then the sum of adjusted population counts from each of the poststrata represented in the smaller area gives the adjusted count for that area. Synthetic estimation is therefore a simple method that assumes that for each poststratum, the undercoverage rate is constant across the area for which the adjustment factor is estimated. Although this assumption can only be approximately true, the synthetic estimates still should be more accurate than direct estimates at low levels of aggregation, since direct estimates would be based on very small samples. Synthetic estimation also has the somewhat conservative property that the adjustment for a poststratum in a small area is never more extreme than that estimated for the poststratum in a larger area, unlike some regression methods that can extrapolate beyond the range of values estimated directly.

To smooth the adjustment factors for poststrata defined within substate regions, the Census Bureau (see Farber et al., 1998) is considering use of a raking ratio adjustment. This methodology is described here as it might be applied at the state level in 2000. (This approach was tested in the 1998 census dress rehearsal, though it differed in some details from the decennial application because of the small geographic areas of the dress rehearsal sites.) Each state is divided into several geographical subregions and several sociodemographic population groups (defined by such variables as race, age, and tenure). For each poststratum, defined as the intersection of a population group and a subregion, a separate dual-system estimate is calculated. Because these direct estimates are based on small samples and therefore have high sampling variability, they are not

---

[12]This report does not address details of the necessity for producing integral counts for blocks. To do this the Census Bureau has historically made use of a linear programming routine for rounding, and the plans are to repeat this in 2000. The panel did not examine this procedure.

used without modification to adjust population estimates within the poststrata. Instead, they would be combined to obtain direct estimates for subregions and for statewide population groups. Next, a model is fitted that calculates an adjustment factor that is the product of a factor for the subregion and one for the population group. These factors are calculated so that the total population for each subregion and for each (statewide) population group agrees with the corresponding directly estimated total. (This is often referred to as iterative proportional fitting. Technically, a log linear model for adjustment factors is fit to the population data.) The poststratum adjustment factors are used in synthetic estimation as described above, which preserves consistency with direct estimates for substate regions and statewide sociodemographic groups.

The combination of synthetic estimation and raking is a reasonable approach to substate estimation, especially under the constraint that there can be no sharing of information across states. Alternatives to this approach include empirical Bayes regression models, which were used in 1990 when there was no effort to have state-only estimates. (Observation of this constraint in this case would require 51 different regression models.) This approach required the use of variance smoothing models that were the subject of some debate. One advantage of this approach was the easy incorporation of additional covariates (possibly) predictive of census undercoverage. While this (and other) alternative methods have some advantages over the current planned approach, the panel agrees with the decision of the Census Bureau to use the relatively well-understood set of methods for the 2000 census.

Estimates (especially for small areas) can be affected to some extent by the details of the approach to modeling adopted by the Census Bureau, including the definition of substate geographic areas and demographic groups. The panel urges the Census Bureau to give high priority to research that will permit an early statistically based decision on these detailed issues in time for the 2000 census to conform with prespecification to the extent possible.

In the long run, a wider range of models should be considered for use in future censuses. This research should consider the possibility that, even if state estimates are required to be direct, estimation for substate areas might be improved by using models that pool some information across states, as discussed above.

> **Recommendation 3.9: The panel endorses the proposal to use raking ratio estimation to obtain substate estimates. Research should continue to define the poststrata and geographic regions as quickly as possible for the 2000 census and to examine alternative modeling options for use in 2010.**

A TRANSPARENT HOUSEHOLD FILE

In 1990 there was no attempt to estimate the household characteristics of those persons added based on the PES; they were instead assigned to special quarters of unrelated persons. This procedure presents two problems. First, census data users need to know population characteristics on a household basis. Second, a household file then does not reflect the fact that many households are counted incorrectly in the initial census enumeration. Consequently, the Census Bureau has worked to develop methods to produce a household data file that is consistent with the official person counts produced by integrated coverage measurement, while assigning all persons to realistic households.

Isaki et al. (1997) propose a method for adjusting the frequency of household types in an area to produce person counts consistent with those obtained from dual-system estimation. The procedure uses two inputs: estimated counts by an age/race/ethnicity/sex/tenure category for a state (or substate area) and frequency of household types defined by the number and characteristics of the inhabitants within the census enumeration for the same area. This method produces adjustment factors for each household type such that the distribution of person characteristics for the adjusted household file matches almost exactly those from dual-system estimation.

Because many sets of household adjustment factors could duplicate the estimated person counts, an additional criterion is needed. Isaki et al. selected a set of factors that essentially minimize the change in the distribution of household types according to a simple mathematical criterion. They evaluated their methodology on 1995 test census data from both the Paterson, New Jersey, and the Oakland, California, sites using 42 person categories and about 350 household types.

This model "weights up" households at a rate that depends on the number of members of undercounted groups that are in a household, which does not necessarily correspond to underestimation of the number of households of that detailed type. There are two potential problems with this methodology. First, it might distort the distribution of household types at low levels of aggregation. For example, if dual-system estimation demonstrates that young adult males were substantially undercounted, the method might increase the number of households consisting of several young men even if the undercount resulted from missed enumerations in other types of households. Similarly, the method might need to delete some households consisting of person types that were counted accurately (e.g., elderly females) to compensate for similar persons added in other household types. Second, even if the correct adjustment factors are known, using them might have unintended effects that would disturb the person counts for small areas. For example, if a certain type of person (i.e., in a particular poststratum) is heavily under-counted, the households with large numbers of that person type will tend to be weighted up and those with few or none will tend to be weighted down. If the households with multiple persons of that type are concen-trated in certain areas, those areas would be given additional population at the expense of others where households have few members of that type. This would not agree with the synthetic estimates for those areas. A similar situation could arise if the people in the undercounted group fall into the same households as people of an overcounted group in one area but are in separate households in another area. While there is no way to know for sure whether one set of estimates is superior at this level of aggregation, the synthetic estimates derived directly from estimated person counts are based on assumptions that the panel thinks are more plausible.

This potential discrepancy for small-area counts could be eliminated or reduced greatly by controlling person-type counts for areas much smaller than a state. However, that modification might inordinately in-crease the range of household-type adjustment factors and, consequently, have a greater potential to distort the distribution of household types.

The difficulty in deciding between various approaches is mainly a result of the limited amount of information used from dual-system esti-mation about attachment of person types to households. Because there is no guarantee that these problems can be addressed adequately by 2000, the Census Bureau has decided not to produce a household data file as part of the official census 2000 products. Instead, imputations (in all census data products) used to account for the undercounted population will have a special nonhousehold category designation used for house-hold characteristics. The panel concurs with this decision but also believes the Bureau should continue to address this important issue. Ac-curate assignment of persons to households would benefit from direct evidence about the types of assignment errors made in the basic census enumeration and about the true distribution of household types. The panel encourages the Census Bureau to conduct research on methods for using integrated coverage measurement to estimate the frequency of household-type assignment errors. The panel is aware of recent work on the transparent file that addresses many of the above concerns and strongly supports research in this direction. The panel also urges that a transparent file be produced from the 2000 census for research use.

Finally, placement of integrated coverage measurement additions into a special nonhousehold category serves to compromise the goals of a "one-number" census, since it makes unadjusted counts easy to construct.

This is additional strong motivation to address this problem before the next census.

> **Recommendation 3.10: The panel concurs with the decision of the Census Bureau not to use a transparent file to provide household assignments for persons added through use of integrated coverage measurement in the 2000 census. However, the Census Bureau should continue research on production of public-use files that are consistent for persons, housing units, and households, along the lines of current research on a transparent file. Considerable effort should be taken to avoid use of a special nonhousehold category in the 2010 census.**

4

Evaluation of Some Common Arguments Against ICM-Based Adjustment of the Census

This chapter addresses in detail a number of issues in the statistical research literature that raise important concerns as to whether integrated coverage measurement (ICM) should be used in the 2000 census. This substantial statistical literature—especially portions of *Survey Methodology* for June 1992, the *Journal of the American Statistical Association* for September 1993, and *Statistical Science* for November 1994—specifically addresses the questions of whether to use adjusted counts for the 1980 and 1990 censuses. It contains analyses that both support and oppose the panel's position, that is, that use of integrated coverage measurement in the 2000 census will in all likelihood result in counts that are preferable to the "unadjusted" counts for key uses of census data.[1] In this chapter the panel discusses the results and arguments presented in this literature, providing a detailed argument supporting the panel's position on the likely effectiveness of integrated coverage measurement in the 2000 census. We stress that this chapter is not concerned with issues that might arise in the field operations necessary to support integrated coverage

---

[1]For ease of presentation the term "adjustment" and related terminology are used in referring to the 1980, 1990, and the 2000 censuses. However, to be more accurate, the terminology related to integrated coverage measurement should be used in referring to the 2000 census, since the plan is to provide one set of counts by the end of 2000. When the term "unadjusted" counts is used regarding 2000, it does not mean that sampling was not used in the census, since sampling for nonresponse follow-up might be used in producing the counts. Instead, it would simply mean that integrated coverage measurement was not used to determine the final census counts.

measurement, except that we do make the assumption that field operations supporting matching in 2000 will be at least as successful as they
were in 1990.

The substantial statistical literature highlights three specific concerns
related to the use of census adjustment: (1) matching error and the bias
from imputation of match status for unresolved cases, (2) unmodeled
heterogeneity in census undercoverage for lower levels of geographic
aggregation (violation of the so-called synthetic assumption), and (3) correlation bias, and the heterogeneity of probabilities of enumeration of
individuals in the census and the integrated coverage measurement survey.[2] These concerns are related to potential failures of the statistical
assumptions that underlie the integrated coverage measurement estima-
tors. Such assumptions are used only as approximations to the truth
(which can never be known), and so the relevant point is not whether
these assumptions obtain exactly but the extent to which they do and do
not apply and the resulting effects on the quality of the adjusted census
counts in comparison with the quality of the unadjusted counts.

Before proceeding, we must consider how one might assess whether
adjusted counts are preferred to unadjusted counts, or, more generally,
how any one set of estimated counts is preferred to another. In general,
the "closer" a set of counts is to the true counts, the better. There are a
variety of measures of disparity, known as loss functions, that measure
how "close" a set of estimated counts is to the true counts. These loss
functions are defined so that smaller values indicate more accurate counts.
The many possible loss functions represent different uses of the data and
varying notions of the costs of disparities. For example, the apportion-

---

[2]There are other concerns that we do not examine in this chapter. One is that a substantial data processing error in the initial computations for the 1990 post-enumeration survey
has raised arguments that the ICM methodology is complex and therefore prone to error.
There is always a chance for human error in data processing and computation, and the risk
is somewhat larger with integrated coverage measurement than without. However, the
panel believes that the risk is relatively low for the 2000 census given the testing that has
already taken place and that is going on in the 1998 census dress rehearsal. A second
concern is that the use of a post-enumeration survey (PES) does add sampling variance that
can be noticeable at the level of the poststrata, and this additional variability can result in
some adjusted counts for individual poststrata being inferior to unadjusted counts. In
response, adjustment will likely improve accuracy overall even if the estimates for a minority of poststrata are made worse. Increasing the sample size of the post-enumeration survey, as is planned for 2000, reduces this problem, and increasing the number of poststrata
worsens it, but in that case smoothing (which can mean various procedures) can reduce the
additional variability at the poststratum level. Of course, the important estimates are not
estimates for poststrata but estimates for areas, which are functions of the estimates for
poststrata.

ment formula for the U.S. House of Representatives can be interpreted as minimizing a certain loss for the discrepancy between the fraction of the population in each state and the fraction of the representatives they are granted (see Balinski and Young, 1982). Since the census is used at different levels of aggregation, loss functions are also applied at different levels of aggregation, such as states, counties, or school districts. Two examples of loss functions are the weighted sum of squared deviations of estimated county counts from true county counts, where the weights might be the inverse of population size, or the sum of absolute deviations of estimated state shares from true state shares.

Given the many uses of census counts, it is unlikely that in comparison of two reasonable sets of estimates, all of the relevant loss functions would find one set of counts superior to the other. However, some uses of the census counts, such as reapportionment, are generally considered of particularly great importance, and it makes sense to consider the loss functions associated with those uses. Most of the key uses of census counts are to allocate a "fixed pie," and therefore loss functions that measure how close the estimated *shares* are to the true shares at some level of geographic aggregation are more important than loss functions that measure how close the estimated counts are to the true counts.

No one can directly measure loss since a set of true counts does not exist. Therefore, to assess whether loss is greater for one set of counts or shares than another, indirect means are needed.

MATCHING ERROR AND THE BIAS FROM IMPUTATION OF MATCH STATUS FOR UNRESOLVED CASES

The panel recognizes that bias was present from a variety of sources in both the adjusted and the unadjusted census counts in 1990 and that bias will be present again in the counts from the 2000 census, whether or not ICM information is used to "adjust" the 2000 census. The panel emphasizes that the statistical term "bias" refers to the fact that an estimator is, on average, higher (or lower) than the quantity it is intended to estimate. As used here, "bias" carries no connotation of prejudice or manipulation. The key inputs to a decision of whether to use integrated coverage measurement should be estimates of the size of the biases and variances to which the two competing sets of counts are subject. The most useful framework in which to compare adjusted and unadjusted counts is the total error model, used by Mulry and Spencer (1991, 1993; see also Zaslavsky, 1993), in which all biases and variances of the competing counts can be accounted for by measuring their effect on a selected loss function.

All evidence from previous censuses suggests that the unadjusted census contains substantial biases. Adjusted counts will retain some bias while adding variance through the use of PES sample-based information. Even without use of the total error model, there is evidence that supports the panel's position—that is, that the remaining bias is likely to have a limited effect on the estimated undercount. One source of potential bias that has received particular attention is matching error, including the bias from imputation of match status for unresolved matches.

Matching plays a key role in dual-system estimation. Errors from matching must be minimized, since bias from matching error of the order of just a few percentage points would be of the same order as differential undercount and therefore make it difficult to support the use of integrated coverage measurement. The amount of matching error and bias and variance from the imputation of unresolved match status (actually match probability) must be factored into any decision on the use of integrated coverage measurement. To support integrated coverage measurement, one must be convinced that the amount of matching bias and variance is small enough that the adjusted counts are still more accurate than the unadjusted counts. (Assessment of the effect of matching error in combinations with other sources of bias is then conducted using a total error model.)

A post-enumeration survey has two main components—the P-sample and the E-sample. The P-sample consists of households found by the post-enumeration survey in PES blocks; the E-sample consists of census enumerations for PES blocks. P-sample matches (matches of P-sample households to the census) are key to estimating the rate of census gross undercoverage. P-sample matching error arises from the incorrect determination of which persons in the ICM survey can be matched to persons in the census enumeration. E-sample matches are key to estimating the rate of erroneous enumeration. E-sample matching error is due to the incorrect determination of which forms collected in the census enumeration are erroneous enumerations. Both P- and E-sample matching have three stages: (1) a computer match of a large fraction of the sample (expected to be at least 80 percent for both samples for 2000); (2) a clerical match of most of the remainder, with field follow-up of unresolved matches to collect more information to reduce the number of unresolved cases; and (3) imputation of match status for unresolved matches. (The clerical match is often assisted by potential matches suggested by the computer matching algorithm.) A great many instances of unresolved match status are due to inability to collect adequate information on a household (including the address) or on the people at an address.

In the 1990 P-sample, interviews were not obtained from 1.2 percent of the households, and 2.1 percent of the individuals in interviewed households had unresolved match status because of incomplete information

(Belin and Diffendal, 1991; Belin et al., 1993). Only 0.9 percent of the E-sample had unresolved match status (Ericksen et al., 1991). Logistic regression models were used in 1990 to impute match probability for unresolved cases for both the P- and the E-samples. (Some of the theory underlying these models and assessments of the variability they add to adjusted counts can be found in Belin et al., 1993.) Although simpler imputation methods are planned for the 2000 census to substitute for the use of logistic regression, the argument that this source of error will remain limited in 2000 is similar given the sensitivity analysis work cited below.

Given that at least 3 percent of P-sample cases in 1990 had unresolved match status, an inadequate imputation model would make it difficult to use integrated coverage measurement. (It is also important to check if there were subgroups for which the percentage with unresolved match status was not substantially larger than the overall rate; otherwise, the estimates for a subgroup could be poor.) However, the available evidence indicates that the imputation models worked well. Belin et al. (1993) describe the Census Bureau's effort to validate the P-sample imputation model. The Bureau carried out an evaluation follow-up interview study in which 11,000 households in a sample of evaluation blocks were reinterviewed to collect all data on address errors, non-interviews, and so forth, to resolve their enumeration status. (Given the distance in time from census day, it was successful in resolving enumeration status for only slightly more than 40 percent of households.) In this study, 31.6 percent of households were determined to have been enumerated in the 1990 census. The mean probability of enumeration imputed for these cases using the logistic regression model was 32.2 percent, which compares extremely well with the survey results. This is solid support for the use of the imputation model for P-sample match status. Given the extent of nonresponse in the evaluation follow-up interviews, it is not conclusive evidence, but it is strong evidence against concern that the imputation model was seriously wrong. Furthermore, the work of Mulry and Spencer (1991, 1993), based on the research of Mack (1991), demonstrates that the use of reasonable alternative match status (probability) imputation routines would not have appreciably changed the adjusted census counts in 1990. Therefore, the contribution to loss from misspecification of the logistic regression model is likely small.

The remaining concern involving matching is the frequency of individuals who were assigned matches that were not true matches, or vice versa. The concern that matching error could be the source of an appreciable bias is reasonable because (1) clerical matching involves an element of judgment, even though it is carried out following standardized procedures, and (2) there are more opportunities to mistakenly declare a matching case to be a nonmatch than to mistakenly declare a nonmatch to be a match, possibly resulting in too high an estimate of the number of nonmatches. (However, given the liberal use of unresolved status, this may be less asymmetric than it appears.) This would give the estimate of undercount a positive bias.[3]

There were two primary sources of information on matching error from 1990. The first source was the Matching Error Study (Davis et al., 1991, 1992), which involved a dependent rematch of a subsample of 919 block clusters (71,000 P-sample cases), where the rematch was conducted by more highly skilled personnel with more time than those who worked in the census. The term "dependent rematch" indicates that the decisions previously made by clerks during the 1990 census were known to the rematch staff. The results of these studies indicate that the estimated bias in the P-sample match rate for 10 or 13 evaluation poststrata (depending on the study) was only significantly different from zero for one or two poststrata. (We have argued elsewhere for the use of loss functions to make these types of assessments.) The potential effect of this bias on the dual-system estimation counts in one of these two studies was to overestimate the population in these two evaluation poststrata by 1.3 and 0.7 percent, respectively, which was substantially below the amount of net undercount (6.8 percent and 4.0 percent, respectively) for the associated groups in the census (see Mulry and Spencer, 1993).

Breiman (1994) focuses attention on the disagreement rates from this study: he points out that for P-sample cases the average disagreement rate across enumeration strata between the original match status and that of the rematch staff for those cases originally classified as unresolved matches, weighted to the total population, was 23.8 percent.

Although the Breiman result is certainly higher than one would like, it is not particularly disturbing. First, the unresolved matches are a relatively small fraction of the total population. This is clear from the fact that the overall disagreement rate estimated as a fraction of the total population is 1.8 percent. Also, the number of P-sample matches in the rematching study, weighted to the total population, differs from the number in the census production matching by only 0.18 percent. The difference appears because disagreement rates do not allow for offsetting errors.

---

[3]All of the studies that the panel is aware of have repeatedly demonstrated that the computer match itself, which does not attempt matches on "problem" cases, has a very small error rate. Therefore, the great majority of errors were committed in the clerical match stage. Belin and Rubin (1995) point out that the software can now be set up so that an estimated error rate is an input parameter, allowing the program to be more or less conservative as to how much agreement is needed to define a match.

That is, for a poststratum, one erroneous match and one erroneous non-match cancel each other out, so disagreement rates do not translate directly into bias estimates. Finally, some of the individual disagreements would occur when the rematch produced either a match or a nonmatch, when one would surmise that the imputation routine for an unresolved case often produced a probability of match that was either, respectively, very high or very low, which would be essentially an agreement.

The second source of information on the quality of the matches in 1990 is from Ringwelski (1991). After some clerical matching in 1990 was completed, the more difficult matching was processed by two different teams, designated SMG1 and SMG2, which worked independently of each other. Though all cases of disagreement proceeded to an oversight match group, the disagreement rate between SMG1 and SMG2 was about 10 percent, which indicates less reliability than one would desire in the clerical match of difficult cases. The specific disagreement rates, discussed by Breiman (1994), were 10.7 percent for matches, 6.6 percent for nonmatches, and 31.2 percent for unresolved cases. However, this again is presumably an overestimate of the extent of the problem since a large fraction of cases involved one match group designating a case as a match and the other group designating the same case as unresolved, where the unresolved case (possibly frequently) could have been given an imputed match status probability of close to 1.0, thereby contributing little to differences in estimated undercount. Furthermore, it must be understood that this result involves only 10 percent of less than 25 percent, or less than 2.5 percent of the cases; it does not directly measure matching error; and it does not allow for offsetting errors.

The 2000 census could be subject to increases in matching problems, since large increases in the percent of individuals that use "Be Counted" forms in 2000 over the percent that used "Were You Counted" forms in previous censuses would be problematic, and there could be substantially increased difficulties in matching due to use of PES-C or PES-A rather than PES-B.[4] It might be sensible to behave as if "Be Counted" would continue to be a relatively small number of additions, based on the experience of the test censuses, but the problems from use of PES-A or PES-C are harder to assess a priori (see discussion in Chapter 3).

In summary, assuming that matching methods in the 2000 census are even modestly improved over those used in 1990, and assuming that changes in census procedures since 1990 do not add substantial new chal-

---

[4]PES-A, PES-B, and PES-C are various methods for treating the matching of movers as part of a post-enumeration survey and dual-system estimation; see the discussion in Chapter 3.

lenges to matching, matching is unlikely to have a substantial effect on the resulting adjusted population counts. To measure more directly the effect of matching error on adjusted counts, matching error studies for 2000 should try to directly estimate loss, rather than use hypothesis tests, on both a count and a share basis, at the state level and substate levels of interest, in order to measure the effect of matching error on adjusted counts.

UNMODELED HETEROGENEITY IN CENSUS UNDERCOVERAGE FOR LOWER LEVELS OF GEOGRAPHIC AGGREGATION

Direct estimates of census undercoverage will exist in 2000 (roughly) at the level of the poststrata, which represent relatively large levels of geographic and demographic aggregation, likely on the order of hundreds of thousands of individuals. In 1990, 1,392 poststrata were initially used for a small PES sample, and 357 poststrata were later used for purposes of examining adjustment for intercensal estimation. The precise number of poststrata for the 2000 census has not been determined, but the need to produce direct state estimates (so all poststrata are defined within state boundaries) will cause, everything else being equal, the number of poststrata to increase relative to 1990. However, the more poststrata, the more variable are the poststrata estimates of undercoverage. These two considerations will likely result in 500 to 1,000 poststrata. Once these direct estimates are made, synthetic estimation and iterative proportional fitting are planned to be used in 2000 to produce estimates at the lowest levels of aggregation (i.e., blocks) consistent with (summing to) the higher level direct estimates.

Clearly, these undercoverage estimates at very low levels of aggregation must derive from direct estimates of much larger aggregates. As a result, a second critical argument often put forth is that while the adjusted census counts are likely better at the original levels of geographic and demographic aggregation (i.e., at the level of poststrata), the adjusted counts are inferior to the census counts at much lower levels of aggregation. The panel argues above that the performance of estimated counts at very detailed levels of geographic aggregation (say, blocks and block groups) is not critical since the key uses of decennial census counts are for purposes such as apportionment, redistricting, fund allocation, and public and private planning, which typically make use of census counts at higher levels of aggregation. The estimates at lower levels of aggregation are used primarily as "building blocks." However, there are some uses of census counts at lower levels of aggregation than the poststrata, so it is important to determine whether adjusted counts are at least as good as unadjusted counts at lower levels of aggregation. The panel finds two arguments that support this point. First, as Tukey (1983) demonstrates, assuming that it has been established that adjusted counts are preferred at a higher level of geographic aggregation in a single poststratum, adjusted counts (not aggregated over demographic groups) produced by synthetic estimation will also be preferred for all lower levels of geographic aggregation. Here, the term "preferred" reflects that they have lower loss, determined through use of a specific loss function for population counts.[5]

As an example, assume that there are three areas, A, B, and C, where the aggregate census count is 180 and the adjusted count is 192. Assume that the census counts of areas A, B, and C are 30, 60, and 90, respectively. The adjusted counts at this level of aggregation using synthetic estimation would be 32, 64, and 96, allocating the 12 additional people in proportion to the census counts. Even if the entire undercounted population happened to reside in area A, it is still the case that the adjusted counts would have less loss and therefore be preferred to the unadjusted counts. (In this case the contribution to loss from this poststratum for adjusted counts is 3.05; for the census counts it is 3.43.) Since we have only represented the case for a single poststratum, we cannot demonstrate the contributions to a share loss function. This is discussed below.

The advantages of synthetic estimation have also been examined through use of simulations at the state level by Schirm and Preston (1987, 1992). Using an empirical approach, they demonstrated that counts produced using synthetic estimation were preferred to unadjusted census counts in a wide variety of simulated circumstances. The benefits are acknowledged to be relatively modest—which is only to be expected since no new information is being provided at that level of aggregation—but the preference for adjusted counts to unadjusted counts occurs with relatively high probability. Using results based on the 1990 census, Hartigan (1992) also found that synthetic adjustment is likely to help.

In two respects these analyses do not settle the issue. First, synthetic estimates used for adjustment are aggregated over poststrata to produce estimated counts for small areas. As pointed out by National Research Council (1985), when the results of synthetic estimation are aggregated over demographic poststrata to produce small-area estimates, the optimality theorem demonstrated by Tukey no longer holds, and examples can be created in which unadjusted counts are preferred to the adjusted ones. However, such counterexamples are difficult to construct and are probably relatively rare. It would require, for example, that the

---

[5]The specific loss function used is $\sum_i (y_i - t_i)^2 / t_i$, where y_i denotes an estimated count, and t_i denotes the true count, for area i, denoting units at some level of geographic aggregation of interest.

undercount for an undercounted group is less in areas where the group is more concentrated (see Schirm and Preston, 1992), which is contrary to anecdotal evidence that extreme undercounts occur in areas with the most concentrated problems.

Second, the simulation results from Schirm and Preston and Hartigan, as well as Tukey's results, assume that the adjusted estimates for the poststrata have less error than the corresponding unadjusted estimates. A more complete and realistic simulation would assume that estimates for various poststrata are subject to error of various magnitudes probabilistically, and then see whether synthetic estimation does result in counts with reduced loss as measured by typical loss functions.

The research by Wolter and Causey (1991), which partially addresses this point, provides the second and more compelling defense of adjustment at low levels of aggregation. They investigated the problem of when adjustment would be preferred at various levels of aggregation (state, county, and enumeration district), assuming that adjusted counts are unbiased for the truth. Given some assumptions about the distribution of the errors, Wolter and Causey (1991:284) found:

> For future censuses, we believe that the following may be a good rule of thumb: Census correction is worthwhile within a stratum if the actual CV [coefficient of variation] of the external estimator of total population is less than the true census undercount rate. For perspective, we note that the Census Bureau's 1990 post-enumeration survey will include about 150,000 housing units, achieving a sampling CV of about 1.4 percent in each of about 100 sampling strata. Total CV's for the 1990 post-enumeration survey will include the 1.4 percent, plus various additions because of nonsampling error . . . and minus various deductions as a result of fitting hierarchical regression models. . . . Thus the level and distribution of original population counts within a stratum will be moved closer to their true values by the correction methods studied here, provided that the actual CV of the post-enumeration survey (designed to be the net of the 1.4 percent plus additions minus deductions) is less than the true undercount rate.

Expanding on this last point, given that the post-enumeration survey for the 2000 census is planned to include 750,000 housing units and assuming 500 poststrata, and assuming that the net of nonsampling error and smoothing is zero additional error, the coefficient of variation in each poststratum would be expected again to be about 1.4 percent. This number is likely to satisfy Wolter and Causey's rule of thumb with respect to expected undercount rates for the 2000 census in poststrata with substantial undercoverage and will otherwise not substantially alter the counts from the census enumeration. If there are 1,000 poststrata, the coefficient of variation would rise to about 2.0 percent.

As pointed out by Schafer (1993), Census Bureau staff are well aware that the "synthetic assumption"—namely, that small areas are homogeneous with respect to their undercoverage properties—is clearly false. Also, Ericksen and Kadane (1991) point out that given the PES sample size and the limited set of variables that are collected on the census short form, the Census Bureau is limited in the number of poststrata that can be formed. So some heterogeneity will exist. However, the question is instead whether the counts resulting from the use of this assumption are inferior to the unadjusted counts with respect to sensible loss functions. The above argument indicates that adjusted counts could very well be preferred at even low levels of aggregation.

Unfortunately, Wolter and Causey's work is based on two assumptions that may limit the applicability of their results. First, the assumption of the unbiasedness of the adjusted counts is clearly not true. Sensitivity analyses should be carried out to examine the effects of the relaxation of this assumption on their results. Second, geographic effects that are not addressed by the poststratification used that affect the degree of census undercoverage could result in higher errors for low levels of geographic aggregation than represented by Wolter and Causey's analysis. Again, some postulated amount of low-level geographic heterogeneity that is not taken care of through poststratification should be incorporated into their analysis to see what the effects might be on adjusted loss in comparison to census loss.

One might ask what the total error model of Mulry and Spencer (1991, 1993) indicates about the error through use of the synthetic assumption. Freedman and Wachter (1994) were concerned that it was misguided since it ignored the effects of the failure of the synthetic assumption on comparisons between adjusted and unadjusted counts. To measure the extent to which this might be true, Freedman and Wachter analyzed proxy variables (variables that are assumed to be related to the variable of interest, e.g., the percentage of people who failed to mail back their census questionnaire and the percentage of people whose entire census records were imputed) for which there is no (or essentially no) sampling variability and for which the extent of the failure of the synthetic assumption could be measured directly. Their analysis found that the Mulry and Spencer analysis was biased against adjustment for six of the eight proxy variables, essentially unchanged for one variable, and biased in favor of adjustment for the remaining variable. Of course, analyses using proxy variables are somewhat dependent on the similarity of the relevant characteristics of the distributions (i.e., the patterns of heterogeneity) of the proxy variables to that of the undercount. However, Freedman and Wachter's analysis suggests that the Mulry and Spencer analysis was not biased in favor of adjustment.

Two additional points are worth noting. First, a hypothesis test used in the CAPE report (Committee on Adjustment of Postcensal Estimates, 1992) tested whether adjusted counts had significantly less loss than unadjusted counts. This test demonstrated that adjusted counts were preferred to unadjusted counts at more aggregate geographic levels, but the test did not demonstrate this preference for lower levels of aggregation, i.e., adjusted counts were not shown to be clearly preferred to unadjusted counts. Use of hypothesis testing in this way is not fully informative as a method for comparing adjusted and unadjusted counts since it treats the two sets of counts very asymmetrically. The converse probably was also true—that is, that unadjusted counts were likely not to have demonstrated to have significantly lower loss than adjusted counts. One can argue that a minor advantage of adjusted counts should be ignored because of the many administrative costs and political complications raised from the use of adjusted counts for official purposes. However, a direct comparison of expected loss, with some acknowledgment of the above additional costs, would be preferable to formal hypothesis testing.

Second, the analyses conducted by Tukey, Schirm and Preston, Hartigan, and Wolter and Causey (cited above), considered both loss functions for population counts and loss functions for population shares. However, the question of improvement for shares or counts does complicate the analysis of the benefits of synthetic estimation.

CORRELATION BIAS AND HETEROGENEITY OF THE PROBABILITIES OF INCLUSION IN DUAL-SYSTEM ESTIMATION

Two kinds of departures from the standard assumptions used in dual-system estimation can cause the resulting estimates to be biased: lack of independence between the event of being enumerated in the census and the event of being enumerated in the post-enumeration survey and correlated heterogeneity (across enumeration systems) in the individual probabilities of being enumerated. While these are conceptually distinct, they both produce the same result—biased estimates.[6] We concentrate here on correlated heterogeneity, which causes the bias referred to as correla-

---

[6]Correlated heterogeneity and dependence have similar effects. Roughly speaking, positive dependence is the situation in which if an individual is enumerated in one system, he or she is also more likely to be enumerated in the other system. Correlated heterogeneity is the situation in which if one has a higher probability of being enumerated in one system, then one also has a higher probability of being enumerated in the other system. Both departures from the standard assumptions result in larger expected population counts in the 1st and 4th cells in comparison with expected population counts under the assumption of homogeneity and independence.

tion bias.[7] The independence assumption, as mentioned above, is supported by the Census Bureau's considerable efforts to ensure that the post-enumeration survey is operationally independent of the census. Dependence cannot be measured at the individual level, and at the aggregate level its effect is fully confounded with correlated heterogeneity of enumeration probabilities.

Some effort has been made to model heterogeneity in enumeration probabilities at the level of individuals (see, e.g., Alho et al., 1993), but these efforts are limited by the information that is collected on census forms. It is generally believed that people do have different probabilities of being enumerated and that these probabilities are a function of various individual characteristics. Furthermore, given the similarities of the census and the post-enumeration survey, it is likely that these characteristics would have a similar effect on census and PES enumeration probabilities, which engenders correlated heterogeneity and results in correlation bias. Some of this bias is reduced through use of poststrata that have people with similar characteristics, who thus have similar probabilities of enumeration. The extent to which correlation bias, widely accepted as the largest source of bias in dual-system estimation when used in the decennial census, remains after poststratification, and the effect of any remaining correlation bias on the relative preference of adjusted to unadjusted census counts and shares is the main topic of this section.

In this section, we often refer to the cells of the 2-by-2 contingency table used in dual-system estimation. The set-up is as follows:

	Post-Enumeration Survey	
Census	In	Out
In	1st	2nd
Out	3rd	4th

The heterogeneity of enumeration probability in the census and the post-enumeration survey is recognized by the Census Bureau, which decided in 1990 to use 1,392 poststrata to minimize heterogeneity in the 1990 census.[8] (Sekar and Deming (1949) advocated use of poststrata for the

---

[7]For a rigorous discussion of extensions to the dual-system estimation model and a precise definition of correlation bias, see Wolter (1986).

[8]The question of heterogeneity is related to the debate over the synthetic assumption above, both involving the extent to which all people in a poststratum behave similarly. But the synthetic assumption debate concerns how to "bring down" a poststratum estimate to lower levels. The issue here concerns the formation of estimates at the poststratum level.

same purpose.) Since the plans to adjust the 1990 census were required to be prespecified and the pattern of heterogeneity could not be examined a priori, the Census Bureau decided to create a relatively large number of poststrata to accommodate whatever heterogeneity patterns might be discovered. Later analysis identified some patterns of similarity among poststrata with respect to undercoverage. Collapsing of poststrata resulted in the final use of only 357 poststrata for purposes of intercensal estimation. The tables in Hogan (1993) indicate that the enumeration probabilities do differ substantially across these poststrata, so the poststrata do account for some heterogeneity. Unfortunately, it is very difficult to measure how much of the total heterogeneity was removed using either the original 1,392 or the later 357 poststrata, but it is safe to conjecture that other variables that were unavailable to the Census Bureau would have further reduced the heterogeneity. Therefore, the panel agrees with Schafer (1993) and Ericksen and Kadane (1991) that the use of poststrata very likely did not eliminate heterogeneity

The only direct evidence on the size and effects of correlation bias is at the national level and is acquired through demographic analysis. (Even at the national level, demographic analysis is subject to error. Attempts are currently being made to quantify this error; see Robinson et al., 1993. Bell (1993) using demographic analysis to estimate the degree of correlation bias, determined that the total of 4th cells for black males aged 20 to 44 in the 1990 census should have been estimated to be around three times larger than the count estimated through assuming homogeneity in the enumeration probabilities. Other demographic groups experienced different degrees of estimated correlation bias.

Even though little is known, at the level of the poststrata, about the effect of heterogeneity on adjusted counts, correlation bias does not negate the superiority of adjusted to unadjusted counts. As shown by Kadane et al. (1999), if the probabilities of enumeration in both the postenumeration survey and the census are positively correlated within poststrata, the adjustment would be biased, but in the right direction. This assumed positive correlation is reasonable since census procedures are similar to PES procedures. Therefore, correlation bias due to heterogeneity of enumeration probabilities is likely to result in dual-system-based estimates that are imperfect but better than no adjustment.

This argument is at least somewhat dependent on the use of a loss function based on population counts, rather than population shares. For "small" adjustments, Taylor series arguments can be made to show that similar benefits would transfer to share loss functions. Also, an estimated undercount that had similar bias across poststrata would clearly be beneficial for share loss functions. However, the first point is not compelling for larger adjustments, and it is unlikely that dual-system estimates have similar bias across poststrata. Further research needs to be carried out as to the effects of correlation bias on loss functions for shares. (Although more theory would be desirable, this question may be more of an empirical than a theoretical one.) A greater understanding of the magnitude of correlation bias in the various poststrata would help to inform a decision as to whether adjusted counts are preferred for share loss functions.

The above argument implicitly assumes that everyone has a non-zero probability of being enumerated in the census and the post-enumeration survey. Some have argued that there is so-called hard undercoverage, individuals who have an enumeration probability equal to zero. Darga (1998) suggests that possibly a great majority of individuals have either a probability of one or zero of being enumerated in the census and the post-enumeration survey. It is possible that at least a close approximation to this problem exists: for example, portions of the homeless population certainly have enumeration probabilities that are very small, if not zero. But this is not a concept that can be rigorously defined. For example, what is often ignored is that some people who refuse to cooperate are still enumerated during last resort through information provided by neighbors, landlords, and postal workers.

We show first that most of census undercoverage is likely 3rd cell undercoverage, those directly measured as missing through use of the post-enumeration survey, as opposed to 4th cell undercoverage, which is estimated through use of the assumption of no correlation bias. Then we demonstrate further why the existence of hard undercoverage is also not a compelling argument against use of adjusted counts.

First, for most poststrata, the size of the estimated 4th cell of the 2-by-2 contingency table is small compared with the size of the estimated 3rd cell—individuals missed by the census enumeration but included in the post-enumeration survey. The ratio of the 3rd cell relative to the estimated 4th cell should be roughly equal to the probability of being enumerated in the post-enumeration survey divided by the probability of being missed in the post-enumeration survey. For 1990, nationally, the sum of the 3rd cells was 18.8 million, while the sum of the 4th cells was 1.5 million (Thompson, 1992). This estimate of 18.8 million 3rd cell enumerations is biased high as an estimate of the number of gross census omissions, since, e.g., census enumerations with insufficient information cannot be matched to the post-enumeration survey, and as a result those people who should have been 1st (or 2nd) cell enumerations become included as 3rd cell enumerations. A relatively unbiased estimate of the number of gross census omissions, as estimated by dual-system estimation, in the 1990 census is 9 million (GAO, 1992).

Clearly, the majority of those added by dual-system estimation are "3rd cell adds," those for whom, in a straightforward sample-based inference, there is direct evidence of their being missed in the census and counted in the post-enumeration survey. (There is also information on individual and household characteristics for these missed people.) Many if not most of these additions must be due to deficiencies in census operation, since the methods used by the post-enumeration survey and the census are relatively similar. This result strongly suggests that deficiencies in census operations are associated with much *measured* census undercoverage.

Furthermore, rough correspondences of counts for historically under-counted groups from dual-system estimation in 1990 with those from demographic analysis suggest the possibility that a majority of all census undercoverage, even that not accounted for by dual-system estimation, is due to 3rd-cell enumerations. For example, in 1990, the PES-estimated undercoverage for blacks was 4.6 percent (Hogan, 1993) while that from demographic analysis was 5.7 percent (Robinson et al., 1993). The difference—undercoverage not measured by the PES—is roughly only one-quarter of what the post-enumeration survey counted. (This argument can be extended nationally to suggest that hard undercoverage is less than 2 million, much less than the estimated 9 million gross census omissions. Estimates derived using this method also could be overestimates since some of the difference between post-enumeration survey and demographic analysis is due to correlation bias.) Therefore, the post-enumeration survey accomplishes what it was (partially) designed to do: measure the extent to which census operations are not perfect. The remaining undercoverage is likely substantially less than the part represented by the 3rd cell. (Of course, improved estimation of the population in the 4th cell is still important.)

Second, what would be the effect on adjusted counts from hard undercoverage? Like the argument with respect to the impact of heterogeneity of enumeration probability, the hard undercoverage problem results in a situation at aggregate levels in which the adjusted counts, while not a perfect solution, are still preferred to the unadjusted census counts using loss functions for population counts.[9] However, it is more difficult to assert the same for a loss function for population shares, which relates to the key uses of census data for apportionment, most fund allocation, etc.

The worry is that the hard undercoverage population could be dis-

---

[9]Only a negative correlation of enumeration probabilities would tend to make the dual-system estimates too high (though high levels of matching error could also have this effect). But given the similarity of the enumeration systems, this seems very unlikely. Positive correlation bias places adjusted counts between the census counts and the true counts, and hence they are preferable to the census counts.

tributed in such a way that shares based on adjusted counts would be inferior to shares based on the census counts. The argument against this reasoning is that there is no characteristic that is known to cause census undercoverage that is also known to be distributed in a strongly nonuniform manner across poststrata. The ethnographic studies that took place in 1988 and 1990 (see Brownrigg and de la Puente, 1993) suggest that the following characteristics are associated with census undercoverage: mobility, language problems, concealment, irregular relationship to head of household, and resistance to government interaction. Some of these characteristics are more prevalent in areas in which the estimated undercount is large. There are no data available to support the hypothesis that hard undercoverage exists and is largest in areas in which estimated undercount is small.

The panel's conclusion, stated broadly, is that one should measure what one can and that, for what cannot be directly measured, it is appropriate to act consistently with the assumption that the part that cannot be directly measured is, at worst, uncorrelated with the part that can be measured. In addition, it seems unreasonable to ignore information about the distribution of a major part of the undercount because there is a hypothetical, unmeasurable, but very likely smaller component that, only if it had a particular (empirically unsupported) distribution, would cause adjusted shares to have greater loss than unadjusted shares.

The more that can be understood about the distribution of the undercounted population, the better informed will be decisions about adjusting the census, especially with respect to loss functions for shares. Efforts to describe census undercoverage in more detail include the research of Hengartner and Speed (1993), who show that the amount of (unexpected) block-level geographic heterogeneity in estimates of census undercoverage is comparable to the amount of demographic (poststrata-explained) heterogeneity. (Of course, census undercoverage at the block level is very indirectly measured, which complicates the interpretation of their findings.) This finding suggests that there could be geographically based clustering of the undercounted population that might reduce the effectiveness of adjustment for share loss functions. (One possibility is that this geographic pattern in undercoverage is due to enumerator effects.) The work of Hengartner and Speed cannot be used to directly compare adjusted and unadjusted counts with respect to a share loss function. Research that directly addresses this issue would be useful.[10]

---

[10]For example, the panel carried out an analysis that showed that, for 1990, roughly 50 percent of the variability of county-level PES-estimated rates of census undercoverage was explained by between-state variability, and the remainder by variability between counties within the same state.

All three issues discussed in this chapter have demonstrated that the criticisms against the use of integrated coverage measurement in the 2000 census involve matters for which more research undoubtedly would be useful and areas for which technical or operational improvement (e.g., with respect to matching) would make the decision to use adjustment more clear. The panel discusses this literature to further support its endorsement of integrated coverage measurement. It argues that these three issues are not sufficiently compelling to shift the panel's position supporting the use of integrated coverage measurement as a reliable method for reducing census differential undercoverage and, more broadly, for improving the quality of census counts for the key purposes for which they are used.

5

Research and Experimentation and Data Collection During the Census

As living arrangements, ethnic composition, attitudes toward government, frequency of moving, availability of enumerators, quality of administrative records, and other factors change nationwide, the methods best suited to enumerating the population of the United States also change. In addition, technological innovations (including statistical methods) provide opportunities to improve census methods. Therefore, a cycle of experimentation and data collection during a census, followed by evaluation, further development, and experimentation and testing between censuses is very important. The decennial census provides a unique opportunity to test new methodologies because of its size and its general level of public awareness and acceptance. Plans for research and experimentation and data collection during the 2000 census are now being finalized. These activities begin the process of developing methodologies for 2010.

ROLE OF RESEARCH AND EXPERIMENTATION

The Census Bureau used four criteria in evaluating proposals for research and experimentation during the 2000 census. The research (1) must require the census as the test environment, (2) must provide measurable results, (3) must not compromise the success of the census, and (4) should provide information that will assist in planning major components of future censuses. Furthermore, it was recommended that the research minimize adverse effects on respondents and enumerators, provide significant potential benefits, and introduce no or only minor additional burden to respondents. The current budget for the 2000 census

86

allocates $21 million for research, roughly 0.5 percent of the cost of the census. The panel endorses these criteria and notes that the research budget seems reasonable. The first recommended criterion is extremely important. Research experimentation and data collection should not disturb field operations. Enumerators already have a difficult job, and additional research programs or data collection that complicate their procedures should not be taken on without serious consideration of the benefits and costs. Expanding on the third recommended criterion, the panel also strongly believes that methods that are tested during the census should produce data that are comparable with those collected under current census methodology. Given the use of census data for congressional apportionment and redistricting and the allocation of federal funds, it would be unfair if some areas were penalized or helped by being chosen for census testing.

A concern with respect to testing as part of the decennial census is whether it is possible to predict 12 years in advance of a census (through other testing and experimentation) what methodologies might be effective. After all, technologies change at a rapid pace, and the population itself is dynamic. In response, it is worth noting that in previous censuses, the Census Bureau staff carried out tests that proved useful in advancing census methodology for subsequent censuses. One example is the mailout/mailback procedure, which was tested in 1960 and introduced on a broad scale in 1970. Another is the current testing (initiated in the early 1990s) of various ways to increase response—through redesigning the questionnaire, use of reminder cards, and sending replacement questionnaires—which will likely save substantial funds. The long lead time from one census to the next can actually be beneficial for these changes, since the introduction of a major change to census methodology can have unintended effects on other parts of the census process, and understanding those effects can take a long time and a good deal of careful research.

When unanticipated problems arise during a decennial census that require additional funds, field staff, or other resources, there is an understandable tendency to shift resources from research experimentation and data collection to solving immediate problems. Unfortunately, this may "mortgage the future" of census taking for short-term benefits. Some important issues involving the methodology to be used for the 2000 census would have been clarified if additional data collection had been incorporated into the 1990 census. The Panel on Decennial Census Methodology (which examined census methodology prior to the 1990 census) called specifically for data collection during the 1990 census that the present panel believes would have been useful in planning the 2000 census methodology. A report from that panel (National Research Council, 1988:2-3) states the following:

The panel supports the concept of a master trace sample (MTS) that will facilitate a wide range of detailed studies on the quality of the 1990 census content. As the panel understands the Census Bureau proposal, the MTS will comprise a sample of census records that include not only the final values for each questionnaire item, but also the values for these items at each step in the processing, along with additional information such as whether the respondent mailed back a filled-in questionnaire or responded to telephone or personal follow-up. . . . We applaud the objectives of the MTS and support having as much of the file content as possible available in a public-use format. Such a file would greatly facilitate error analyses of the census. It would support more definitive studies than proved possible for many REX [research, evaluation, and experimental] projects in the 1980 census, in which analysts frequently encountered incomplete and inconsistent field data. . . . One additional application of the MTS that we support is a study of the potential of sampling in the final stages of follow-up to improve the quality of the data. This study would require the capture of data from enumerator records on how many callbacks, by phone and in person, were attempted before an interview was obtained. We understand that these records are not generally well maintained and are for the enumerators' own use. We urge that, for at least a subsample of the MTS, the Census Bureau make an effort to have the enumerators keep good records. These data should then be analyzed to determine the value of sampling.

Unfortunately, due to budget and time constraints, a master trace sample was not collected in 1990.

As in 1990, in 2000 there will be pressures to reduce the number of research experiments, and associated data collection, undertaken during the decennial census. The panel takes this opportunity to suggest priorities for the research experiments, so that if some reductions become necessary, the most promising experiments can be protected. In addition, the fact that nonmonetary resources are constrained during a decennial census argues for focusing on a select number of projects. This concern was expressed by the Panel on Decennial Census Methodology (National Research Council, 1988:3) as another reason for the importance and utility of collecting a master trace sample:

The panel urges that the Census Bureau not include too many separate projects in the REX [research and experimentation] program. Given limited time, staff, and budget resources, it would be far preferable for the Census Bureau to conduct a smaller number of studies well than to attempt a larger number of studies with poor results. In this regard, one advantage of devoting the necessary resources for obtaining a comprehensive and high-quality master trace sample is that the file has the potential for long-range use. It could be analyzed in many different ways throughout the next decade as new ideas and hypotheses about the factors involved in census data quality arise.

The panel notes a final and more general point on the role of research. The 2000 census presents many opportunities for data collection that would be useful to implement to improve census methodology and operations for future censuses. The benefits of experimentation during the census are considerable but are more limited and often carry some risk. Therefore, the first priority should be to understand which data have potential research value and to keep those data in a form that will facilitate later analysis. The second priority is experimentation. In the rest of this chapter we first discuss and assess proposed experiments and then data collection.

PROPOSED EXPERIMENTS AND PANEL'S ASSESSMENT

Seven research experiments have been proposed by the Census Bureau to be carried out during the 2000 census.[1] The panel describes them below in order of our assessment of their priority: high, intermediate, low.

High-Priority Experiments

Alternative Questionnaire and Mail Treatment

This experiment has three parts: (1) the single-page format for the decennial census questionnaire that is currently used would be replaced with a booklet version; (2) a reduced set of residence rules would be used in some questionnaires; and (3) the increase in response from a targeted mailing of a replacement questionnaire would be assessed by an unclustered sample of households. We believe the second and third parts are important. The experiment will provide valuable information on the benefits from a reduced set of residence rules and, more importantly, on the value of a targeted replacement questionnaire in a census environment. The testing of a booklet questionnaire seems less important, since experiments on minor modifications to the questionnaire can be conducted outside the decennial census.

Administrative Records Census Experiment

This test explores whether administrative records could be used to acquire high-quality short-form information through the merging and unduplication of several national administrative records lists. One por-

---

[1]The descriptions of these programs are taken from Keller (1998).

tion of the test would attempt to provide household assignments, while the other would only collect information on individuals. To improve the quality of the match and as a validation tool, a coverage improvement survey would be used to collect both Social Security numbers and reconciliation information. This experiment will help reveal ways in which administrative records could play a more prominent census role, as well as provide various kinds of assistance for the proposed American Community Survey.

The panel supports three modifications that would enhance the value of this experiment. One problem with the current proposal is that none of the national lists target the non-elderly poor, an especially important source of census undercoverage. To remedy this problem, lists of food stamp recipients should be added to the lists already suggested. The panel also questions the allocation of the majority of the costs of this project to the coverage improvement survey, which is needed to provide Social Security numbers for help in matching. Typically, birth dates and names, both generally available on administrative records systems, are sufficient for high-quality matching. It is possible that the coverage improvement survey might help with information on movers. However, the value of the coverage improvement survey should be revisited given its share of the cost. Instead, the coverage improvement survey might be used only as a reconciliation survey, or the funds that are saved through discontinuation of the survey could be used to increase the size of the experimental area.

Finally, this project provides an ideal opportunity to test triple-system estimation: one list would be the census; the second would be the merged administrative records list; and the third would be the integrated coverage measurement survey list. Triple-system estimation offers clear advantages over dual-system estimation (with respect to addressing correlation bias) if the lists are of high quality, and therefore this methodology is worth examining for use as part of integrated coverage measurement in future censuses. Examination of related approaches could also be supported through the collection of these data, including methods for addressing dependence and heterogeneity (e.g., Darroch et al., 1993), as well as work on individual-level models of undercoverage (e.g., Alho, 1990; Huggins, 1989, 1991; Alho et al.,1993).

Use of Administrative Records for Nonresponse Follow-Up

This test would match (by computer) a sample of census nonrespondents with various national administrative records databases to fill in their short-form information. The coverage improvement survey would be used to assess the quality of the information obtained. Discrepancies would be attributed to either the computer match or the quality of the administrative lists. The panel believes that this is an extremely important experiment that could show how administrative records might be used to provide high-quality information and reduce costs in the census.

Targeted Enhancements to the Master Address File

Seven national administrative records lists would be acquired, merged, and unduplicated to produce a single database of addresses. The list would be used to update the master address file (MAF). The hope is to target the field work supporting updating of the MAF to areas with certain identified features, such as large clusters of unmatched street addresses, multiunit structures, blocks where residences have been abandoned, and mobile home parks. Areas to represent widely diverse situations would be selected for study and then subjected to simulated targeted MAF updates. The results for the precanvass operation would be used to conduct cost/benefit studies to compare tradeoffs between reduced fieldwork and loss of coverage in comparison to full canvassing.

The panel is excited about the possibility of using addresses from administrative records to update the MAF for the variety of purposes for which it is intended, including the decennial census. One suggestion is to tie all updates to the Topologically Integrated Geographic Encoding and Referencing (TIGER) system, because an address not referenced to census geography is of limited value.

Intermediate-Priority Experiment

Use of the Employee Reliability Inventory File by Nonresponse Follow-Up Enumerators

This test would use noncognitive tests on candidate enumerators to try to determine which of them have the necessary interpersonal skills for successful job performance, supplementing cognitive tests that will likely be in general use for the 2000 census. The panel is unsure of the value of this test. It is possible that a test of noncognitive characteristics might be useful in reducing employee turnover, but the possible benefits and the likelihood that they would be realized are not clear. However, the costs and risks of this project are minimal, and the project would provide some measurement of enumerator productivity, which is useful.

Low-Priority Experiments

Census Calling Card Incentive Experiment

A sample of all households and a sample of nonresponding households would receive prepaid telephone calling cards (with a value of about $5) along with their questionnaire, with a letter encouraging their response to the questionnaire by telephone. After providing an interview, the calling card would be activated. The panel does not believe that this experiment requires testing during a decennial census. In addition, use of a monetary incentive for what is a legally mandated requirement raises a concern about whether this experiment could be implemented as a regular part of a decennial census.

Social Security Numbers, Privacy Attitudes, and Notification Experiment

To evaluate the degree to which requests for Social Security numbers would be accepted by households, questionnaires would be mailed to a national sample of households to request this information. As an alternative, a sample of census 2000 questionnaires would query respondents on whether they would be willing to provide their numbers. Another part of the experiment would determine the effect on the response rate of a notification on the census form that administrative records will be used to assist the Census Bureau in acquiring information. Finally, the Bureau would make use of a telephone survey to measure broad aspects of current attitudes concerning the computer matching of a household's information.

The panel judges that much of the information gained from this experiment is already in hand, through work on similar issues with respect to household surveys. In addition, it is risky during a decennial census to request information that is not legally required along with information that is so required. This experiment might be successfully conducted during a test census.

Other Experiments

Regarding experiments that were not proposed, the panel has only one suggestion: it might be helpful to test how respondents understand and answer questions regarding their usual place of residence. This concept is still confusing in the draft census instructions (see, e.g., Tourangeau et al., 1997) and will likely lead to substantial reporting errors. The Census Bureau's expectation that a person's residence is the place where he or she lives and sleeps most of the time may not be what is understood by some respondents. However, this expectation could be evaluated during a test census and thus does not require a decennial census environment.

In addition, the panel has some concern that more attention was not devoted to innovative methods for counting hard-to-enumerate populations. Some possibilities might include further work on such ideas as blitz enumeration, where crews of specially trained enumerators work on a compressed time schedule to enumerate an area, and team enumeration, where enumerators work in small groups.

Finally, a study that was described to the panel, the interviewer effects experiment, has been substantially broadened to a 2010 census error modeling and simulation research experiment. The panel did not review this version of the experiment, and so does not provide priorities for its use here.

RECOMMENDATIONS AND SUGGESTIONS FOR DATA COLLECTION

In addition to a setting for experiments, a decennial census is also an opportunity to collect data on current census procedures. Data collection can be even more valuable than research experimentation during a decennial census. Knowing what happened during a census can help identify useful modifications in processes, and data collection can also support simulation studies that assess the benefits of alternative methodologies and identify needs for further research. The panel offers one recommendation and several suggestions for data collection in the 2000 census.

Collection of a Master Trace Sample

The Census Bureau has designed an extremely innovative data collection system to be used during the 2000 census to provide decision support to all operational managers. The data are summarized to support decisions that need to be made in real time. For future analysis, however, detailed process data on individual enumerations will very likely be required. For example, it will undoubtedly be important to know how many interview attempts were made, how long they took, and whether the respondent was a household member or a proxy respondent. Preservation of these data is not required for operational support, and much of this data would not be captured or even recorded by enumerators. Although the Census Bureau is concerned about the cost and additional workload required for collection of this information, the panel believes that it would be worthwhile to collect it on a sample basis. Furthermore, some of these data items could be preserved for research use, again on a sample basis, by designing software systems to abstract these items from the existing data processing system without further enumerator effort.

Therefore, the panel strongly supports a renewal and modest expansion of the suggestion by the Panel on Decennial Census Methodology of 10 years ago (National Research Council, 1988) for the collection of a master trace sample. With the various innovations in the 2000 census, such as the possibility of sampling for nonresponse follow-up and alternative methods for enumeration (e.g., "Be Counted" forms), it would be very useful if the planned data management system could collect a trace sample in, say, 100 census tracts around the country. (Sampling tracts would facilitate study of the effects at the block or interviewer level.) The trace sample would provide information as to what happened in all phases of data collection, which will be instrumental in guiding methodological advances to be used in 2010 and beyond. Specific variables that could be included in the trace sample collection are as follows:

• where the address came from (original master address list, local update, casing check, etc.);
• the type of questionnaire (long or short form), whether, and when it was returned, whether it was the first or a replacement questionnaire (or both), whether respondent-friendly enumeration was (also) used, if the household was a nonrespondent and a member of the nonresponse follow-up sample, then how many approaches for field enumeration were made, when they were they made, which mode was used, whether they were ultimately successful, whether data capture required proxy enumeration and, if so, what type of proxy enumeration, edit failures, and finally whether there were any data differences among duplicate responses for households or individuals; and
• the identification number of the enumerator, to facilitate evaluation of interviewer effects.

Of course, any of the above information that could easily be collected on a 100 percent basis should be.

Additional Suggestions for Data Collection

In addition to the data needed for a trace sample, the following would be valuable to collect:

• All information necessary to estimate the census cost model. This would include the training costs, hourly rate and any other compensation of enumerators, turnover rate, number of hours worked, responses per hour, number of enumeration offices staffed, and how long they were open. This should include costs of all sources of updates to the MAF, and advertising. Linking costs to information on census outcomes (i.e., improvements in the quality of the counts) would make it possible to carry out cost-benefit analyses of the various components of the 2000 census, such as the benefits of the reminder postcard and the replacement questionnaire. (Lack of this information complicated evaluation of the 1990 census and the costing for 2000.)

• A measure of interviewer quality. Information on hiring or training tests might help identify the characteristics of those interviewers who were more skilled, which could be linked to the quality of the data collected.

• The amount and type of duplication and the success of unduplication. The amount of duplication with respect to the various forms of questionnaire response should be measured. On a sample basis, telephone or field follow-up could be used to assess the success of unduplication.

• Complete integrated coverage measurement data. All information pertaining to integrated coverage measurement estimation, including, on a sample basis, integrated coverage measurement interviews, should be collected.

• Data needed to estimate and decompose the variance of the final census estimates. Finally, to be able to use total error modeling in the 2000 census, sufficient information to support such modeling should be collected.

Recommendation 5.1: The panel recommends that a trace sample be collected in roughly 100 tracts throughout the United States and saved for research purposes. The trace sample would collect detailed process data on individual enumerations. In addition, similar information on integrated coverage measurement should be collected, on a sample basis if needed. It would be very useful if information could be collected, again on a sample basis, to support complete analysis of the census costs model, all aspects of the amount of duplication and efforts to unduplicate, and information needed to support total error modeling of the 2000 census.

FINAL NOTE

Our review of the Census Bureau's research and data collection plans was hampered without having the 2000 census evaluation plans. Because they have related objectives, plans for data collection, experimentation, and evaluation need to be considered jointly so that all important issues are covered and there is no unnecessary duplication. Ideally, the

Census Bureau needs to collect all data that support any evaluation studies it intends to carry out. More coordination of these activities would be desirable in the future, by having final evaluation plans earlier. Given the uncertainty about overall census plans and budgets for 2000, however, we recognize why coordination of evaluation and research plans was not possible. We hope that future censuses can benefit from longer times for planning.

Glossary of Relevant Census Terms

Administrative records. Records that are collected as part of the operation of federal, state, and local programs, typically fund allocation and tax programs, such as Internal Revenue Service and Food Stamp Program records.

"Be Counted." A census program that makes census questionnaires available in public places for return, makes census questionnaires available in foreign languages by telephone, and permits responding to the census by telephone.

Casing check. A program in which postal workers determine addresses for which they did not receive a questionnaire and notify the Census Bureau.

Census tract. A census-defined geographic area of roughly 1,500 households.

Closeout. The use in the census of whatever data have been collected by the date by which all interviewing must be concluded. **Imputation** is used to fill in any missing information. See also **Last resort.**

Coefficient of variation. An assessment of the variability of an estimate as a percentage of the size of the quantity being measured.

Computer-Aided Personal Interview (CAPI). The use of a computer to assist an interviewer in carrying out an interview. Advantages include avoiding errors in skip patterns, providing immediate edit checks, and expediting electronic data capture.

Correlation bias. A (technical) bias in **dual-system estimation** by which the estimated counts would be, on the average, either too low or too high, caused by heterogeneity in enumeration probabilities for both the census and the **post-enumeration survey**. The heterogeneities of the probabilities for these two attempted enumerations are typically positively related, which causes the estimated counts to be on the average too low.

Coverage improvement programs. Often (but not always) nationally applied methods and programs that attempt to collect information from individuals and households that might be missed using **mailout/mailback** or **nonresponse follow-up**. Before the 2000 census cycle this term referred to such programs as the parolee and probationer program (used in 1990) in which lists of these individuals were checked to see whether they were enumerated, and the non-household sources program, in which several **administrative record** lists were matched to census records to try to identify people missed in the census for purposes of field follow-up. For the 2000 census, "coverage improvement" refers more to efforts to complete the address list, use of **multiple response modes**, and **service-based enumeration**.

Demographic analysis. A method that uses various **administrative records** (especially birth and death records, information on immigration and emigration, and Medicare records) and information from previous censuses to estimate the total number of people in various demographic groups resident in the United States on a specific date, and therefore their census undercoverage.

Dress rehearsal. The largest census test, typically 2 years before the decennial census, in which the methods and procedures of the upcoming decennial census are given their final test to identify any operational problems.

Dual-system estimation. An estimation methodology that uses two independent attempts to collect information from a household to estimate the number of people missed by both attempts.

Erroneous enumeration. The inclusion of someone in the census in error. Such inclusions may be people born after census day or deceased before census day, people in the United States temporarily, and people in the wrong location. It also includes people counted more than once, i.e., duplicates.

Error. The difference between an estimate and the true value.

Household. All the persons who occupy a **housing unit**.

Housing unit. A house, an apartment, etc., that is occupied (or if vacant, is intended for occupancy) as separate living quarters, which are those in which the occupants live and eat separately from any other persons in the building. See also **household**.

Imputation. A method for filling in missing information. Sequential hot deck imputation fills in information from a previously processed respondent (and therefore geographically close) with other similar characteristics.

Integrated coverage measurement (ICM). The use of a **post-enumeration survey** and some type of estimation method, e.g., **dual-system estimation**, to produce adjusted census counts in time for apportionment and therefore all uses of census data.

Last resort. Last resort enumeration is the collection of data from neighbors, apartment managers, post office employees, etc., and is used when a response from a resident cannot be obtained. See also **closeout**.

Local Update of Census Addresses (LUCA) Program. A Census Bureau program in which local officials are given the opportunity to review address lists and make corrections, additions, and deletions to that list, and to make corrections to census maps to match any changes that may be needed. The LUCA program covers only local governments in **mailout/ mailback** enumeration areas; other local governments are eligible to participate in a different type of address list review program.

Long form. The census questionnaire that is mailed to a (roughly) one-sixth sample of **households** (for **mailout/mailback** areas), which includes the short-form questions and additional questions about income, commuting patterns, etc. See also **short form**.

Mailout/mailback. A method of census enumeration used primarily in urban areas in which questionnaires are mailed to each address and the residents are asked to mail back the completed questionnaires.

Master Address File (MAF). The list of addresses on which the census enumeration is based. It is derived from the 1990 census address list and is updated using a variety of sources, including information from the U.S. Postal Service and local officials. See also **Topologically Integrated Geographic Encoding and Referencing (TIGER) System.**

Matching. The process through which it is determined how many persons are included in both the **post-enumeration survey** and the census (in PES blocks) and how many persons are only included on one or the other attempted enumeration.

Multiple response modes. Generally speaking, methods for being enumerated, not including **mailout/mailback** and enumeration as part of usual **nonresponse follow-up**. In 2000 these methods will include obtaining and returning questionnaires available in public places ("**Be Counted**" forms), the use of the telephone and possibly the internet to obtain or provide census information, and the enumeration of persons at places that offer services to the homeless.

Nonresponse. The failure to obtain all or part of the information requested on a census questionnaire. Mail nonresponse is failure to return the census questionnaire that was mailed to housing units; ICM nonresponse is failure to answer the questions posed by ICM (PES) interviewers.

Nonresponse follow-up. The field operation whereby census enumerators attempt to obtain completed questionnaires from interviewing members of households for which no questionnaire was returned as part of **mailout/mailback**. When done on a 100 percent basis, it is referred to as nonresponse follow-up (NRFU), and when it is done on a sample basis, to distinguish it from NRFU it is referred to as sampling for nonresponse follow-up (SNRFU).

Post-enumeration survey (PES). A sample survey conducted in selected areas after nonresponse follow-up is completed that collects similar information to that collected during the census for purposes of estimating how many people the census undercounted and overcounted; sometimes referred to as a coverage measurement survey. Two separate activities make up the post-enumeration survey: the P-sample is the sample of individuals found by the post-enumeration survey in PES blocks; the E-sample is the sample of census enumerations for PES blocks.

Poststratification. The separating of a data set collected through use of sampling into strata on the basis of information gathered during data collection, and then treating each strata separately in estimation.

Poststratum. A collection (of individuals in the census context) that shares some characteristics (e.g., race, age, sex, region, owner/renter) obtained during data collection and that are separately treated in estimation.

Raking. An estimation procedure in which a table of counts (possibly of several dimensions) is iteratively, multiplicatively adjusted, one dimension at a time, until convergence, so that the resulting table agrees with one-dimensional marginal totals that are considered of higher quality.

Replacement form. A second census questionnaire that is mailed out shortly after the mailing of the reminder card. If the forms are only mailed to initially nonresponding housing units, they are referred to as targeted replacement forms; if they are mailed to all housing units, they are referred to as a blanket replacement forms.

Service-based enumeration. Enumeration of typically homeless people at food kitchens and shelters.

Short form. The census questionnaire that is mailed to about five-sixths of all **households**. The short form concentrates on basic demographic information. See also **long form**.

Topologically Integrated Geographic Encoding and Referencing (TIGER) System. The framework for identifying the exact geographic location of residential addresses (as well as other physical features).

Trace sample (also referred to as master trace sample). A sample of census records (possibly by selecting all records in a sample of decennial census blocks) for which all information relevant to census data collection is retained to assist in analyzing and comparing methodologies suggested for use in the subsequent census.

Transparent file. A file of census enumerations, including those added through the use of **integrated coverage measurement**, which provides household characteristics for the ICM enumerations (and possibly changes in household characteristics for some enumerated in the traditional manner) so that the enumerations added through use of **integrated coverage measurement** are not distinguishable.

UAA vacants. Undeliverable-as-addressed vacants—**housing units** that the postal carrier believes to be vacant, rather than being undeliverable because the address is bad or does not exist.

Under(over)coverage; under(over)count. A nonspecific term representing either the rate or the number of individuals missed (erroneously included) in the decennial census. More specifically, gross undercoverage and gross undercount are the rate or number of those missed for a demographic group or geographic area (similarly for gross overcoverage and gross overcount); net undercoverage and net undercount are the difference between the rate or number of those missed for a demographic group or geographic area and the rate or number of those erroneously included; differential (net) undercoverage and differential (net) undercount are the difference between the rate or number of net undercoverage between two demographic groups or between two geographic areas.

Unduplication. The process by which individuals reported on more than one census questionnaire are identified and counted once at only one geographic location.

Update leave/mailback. A method of census enumeration used primarily in rural areas in which the census questionnaire is delivered to an address by a census enumerator. The **master address file** is corrected at the time of delivery (if necessary). Residents at the address are asked to fill out the questionnaire and mail it back.

References

Alho, J.M.
  1990   Logistic regression in capture-recapture models. *Biometrics* 46:623-635.
Alho, J. M., M.H. Mulry, K. Wurdeman, and J. Kim
  1993   Estimating heterogeneity in the probabilities of enumeration for dual-system esti-
         mation. *Journal of the American Statistical Association* 88:1130-1136
Balinksi, M.L., and H.P. Young
  1982   *Fair Representation: Meeting the Ideal of One Man, One Vote.* New Haven: Yale
         University Press.
Belin, T.R., and G.J. Diffendal
  1991   Results from the Handling of Unresolved Enumeration Status, Missing Character-
         istic Data, and Noninterviews in the 1990 Post-enumeration Survey. STSD Decen-
         nial Census Memorandum Series V 112. Bureau of the Census, U.S. Department of
         Commerce, Washington, D.C.
Belin, T.R., G.J. Diffendal, S. Mack, D.B. Rubin, J.L. Schafer, and A.M. Zaslavsky
  1993   Hierarchical logistic-regression models for imputation of unresolved enumeration
         status in undercount estimation. *Journal of the American Statistical Association*
         88:1149-1159.
Belin, T.R., and J.E. Rolph
  1994   Can we reach consensus on census adjustment? *Statistical Science* 9:486-508.
Belin, T.R., and D.B. Rubin
  1995   A Method for Calibrating False-Match Rates in Record Linkage. *Journal of the Ameri-
         can Statistical Association* 90(430):694-707.
Bell, W.R.
  1993   Using information from demographic analysis in post-enumeration survey estima-
         tion. *Journal of the American Statistical Association* 88(423):1106-1118.
Breiman, L.
  1994   The 1991 census adjustment: Undercount or bad data? *Statistical Science* 9:458-475.

Brown, L.D., M. L.Eaton, D.A. Freedman, S.P. Klein, R.A. Olshen, K.W. Wachter, M.T. Wells, and D. Ylvisaker
  1998 Statistical Controversies in Census 2000. Technical Report No. 537, Department of Statistics, University of California, Berkeley.
Brownrigg, L.A., and M. de la Puente
  1993 Alternative Enumeration Methods and Results: Resolution and Resolved Populations by Site. Bureau of the Census, U.S. Department of Commerce, Washington, D.C.
Bureau of the Census
  1997 Sampling and Estimation in Census 2000 and the Dress Rehearsal. Paper prepared for the Census Advisory Committee of Professional Associations, January 22. Bureau of the Census, U.S. Department of Commerce, Washington, D.C.
  1998a Overview of the Census 2000 Dress Rehearsal Evaluation Program. Paper prepared for the Panel on Alternative Census Methodologies, January 20. U.S. Bureau of the Census, U.S. Department of Commerce, Washington, D.C.
  1998b Census 2000 Dress Rehearsal Mid-Term Status Report. September 1988. Bureau of the Census, U.S. Department of Commerce, Washington, D.C.
Cohen, M.L.
  1989 Synthetic estimation. In *Encyclopedia of Statistical Sciences*, Supplement Volume. New York: John Wiley & Sons.
Committee on Adjustment of Postcensal Estimates
  1992 Assessment of Accuracy of Adjusted Versus Unadjusted 1990 Census Base for Use in Intercensal Estimates. Report of the committee to the Bureau of the Census, U.S. Department of Commerce, August 7, Washington, D.C..
Darga, K.
  1998 Straining Out Gnats and Swallowing Camels: The Perils of Adjusting for Census Undercount. Office of the State Demographer, Michigan Information Center, Michigan Department of Management and Budget.
Darroch, J.N., S.E. Fienberg, G.F.V. Glonek, and B.W. Junker
  1993 A three-sample multiple-recapture approach to census population estimation with heterogeneous catchability. *Journal of the American Statistical Association* 88(423):1137-1148.
Davis, M., M. Mulry, and P. Biemer
  1992 Estimation of matching error in census undercount estimation. In *Proceedings of the Section on Survey Research Methods*. Alexandria, Va.: American Statistical Association.
Davis, M., M. Mulry, R. Parmer, and P. Biemer
  1991 The matching error study for the 1990 post-enumeration survey. Pp. 248-253 in *Proceedings of the Section on Survey Research Methods*. Alexandria, Va.: American Statistical Association.
Ericksen, E.P., and J. Kadane
  1991 Comment on "Total Error in PES Estimates of Population," by M.H. Mulry and B.D. Spencer. *Journal of the American Statistical Association* 86:855-857.
Ericksen, R.P., L.F. Estrada, J.W. Tukey, and K.M. Wolter
  1991 Report on the 1990 Decennial Census and the Post-Enumeration Survey. Report submitted by members of the Special Advisory Panel to the Secretary of the U.S. Department of Commerce, June 21. U.S. Department of Commerce, Washington, D.C.

Farber, J.
  1997 Results of Estimation Research. Internal memorandum dated December 10, for the Statistical Design PSC Team Leaders. Bureau of the Census, U.S. Department of Commerce, Washington, D.C.

Farber, J., R.E. Fay, and E.L. Schindler
  1998 The Statistical Methodology of Census 2000. Bureau of the Census, U.S. Department of Commerce, Washington, D.C.

Fay, R.E, and J.Thompson
  1993 The 1990 post enumeration survey: Statistical lessons, in hindsight. Pp. 71-91 in *Proceedings of the Bureau of the Census Annual Research Conference*. Washington. D.C.: U.S. Department of Commerce.

Freedman, D., and K. Wachter
  1994 Heterogeneity and census adjustment for the intercensal base. *Statistical Science* 9:476-485.

Gbur, P.M.
  1996 1995 Census Test Results: Memorandum No. 44: Integrated Coverage Measurement (ICM) Evaluation Project 3: Noninterview Followup. Bureau of the Census, U.S. Department of Commerce, Washington, D.C.

Gelman, A., J. Carlin, H. Stern, and D.B. Rubin
  1995 *Bayesian Data Analysis*. New York: Chapman and Hall.

Griffin, D.H., and C.L. Moriarity
  1992 Characteristics of census errors. Pp. 512-517 in *Proceedings of the Section on Survey Research Methods*. Alexandria, Va.: American Statistical Association.

Hartigan, J.A.
  1992 Comment on "Should we have adjusted the U.S. census of 1980?" by D.A. Freedman and W.C. Navidi. *Survey Methodology* 19(1):44-50.

Hengartner, N., and T.P. Speed
  1993 Assessing between-block heterogeneity within the post-strata of the 1990 post-enumeration survey. *Journal of the American Statistical Association* 88(423):1119-1125.

Hogan, H.
  1992 The 1990 PES: An overview. *The American Statistician* 46:261-269.
  1993 The 1990 PES: Operations and results. *Journal of the American Statistical Association* 88(423):1047-1060.

Hogan, H., and K. Wolter
  1988 Measuring accuracy in a post-enumeration survey. *Survey Methodology* 14:99-116.

Huggins, R.M.
  1989 On the statistical analysis of capture experiments. *Biometrika* 76:133-140.
  1991 Some practical aspects of a conditional likelihood approach to capture experiments. *Biometrics* 47:725-732.

Isaki, C.T., M.M. Ikeda, J.H. Tsay, and W.A. Fuller
  1997 A Transparent File for a One Number Census. Technical report May 21. Bureau of the Census, U.S. Department of Commerce, Washington, D.C.

Kadane, J.B., M.M. Meyer, and J.W. Tukey
  1999 Yule's association paradox and ignored stratum heterogeneity in capture-recapture studies. *Journal of the American Statistical Association* 94(447).

Keller, J.
  1998 The Census 2000 Research and Experimentation Program. Unpublished memorandum. Bureau of the Census, U.S. Department of Commerce, Washington, D.C.

Mack, S.
   1991   An analysis of the effect of reasonable imputation alternatives on estimates of cov-
          erage error in the 1990 decennial census. Pp. 652-657 in *Proceedings of the Section on
          Survey Research Methods.* Alexandria, Va.: American Statistical Association.
Mulry, M., and B. Spencer
   1991   Total error in PES estimation of population. *Journal of the American Statistical Asso-
          ciation* 86:839-854.
   1993   Accuracy of the 1990 census and undercount adjustments. *Journal of the American
          Statistical Association* 88:1080-1091.
National Research Council
   1985   *The Bicentennial Census: New Directions for Methodology in 1990.* Constance F. Citro
          and Michael L. Cohen, eds. Panel on Decennial Census Methodology, Committee
          on National Statistics, National Research Council. Washington, D.C.: National
          Academy Press.
   1988   *Priorities for the 1990 Census: Research, Evaluation, and Experimental (REX) Program.*
          Panel on Decennial Census Methodology, Committee on National Statistics, Na-
          tional Research Council. Washington, D.C.: National Academy Press.
   1994   *Counting the People in the Information Age.* Duane L. Steffey and N.M. Bradburn,
          eds. Panel to Evaluate Alternative Census Methods, Committee on National Statis-
          tics, National Research Council. Washington, D.C.: National Academy Press.
   1995   *Modernizing the U.S. Census.* Barry Edmonston and Charles Schultze, eds. Panel on
          Census Requirements in the Year 2000 and Beyond, Committee on National Statis-
          tics, National Research Council. Washington, D.C.: National Academy Press.
   1996   *Sampling in the 2000 Census: Interim Report I.* Andrew A. White and Keith F. Rust,
          eds. Panel to Evaluate Alternative Census Methodologies, Committee on National
          Statistics, National Research Council. Washington, D.C.: National Academy Press.
   1997a Letter Report of November 10, 1997, to Dr. Martha Farnsworth Riche. Panel to
          Evaluate Alternative Census Methodologies, Committee on National Statistics, Na-
          tional Research Council, Washington, D.C.
   1997b *Preparing for the 2000 Census: Interim Report II.* Andrew A. White and Keith F. Rust,
          eds. Panel to Evaluate Alternative Census Methodologies, Committee on National
          Statistics, National Research Council. Washington, D.C.: National Academy Press.
   1998   *Small-Area Estimates of Children in Poverty, Interim Report 2, Evaluation of Revised
          1993 County Estimates for Title I Allocations.* Constance F. Citro, Michael L. Cohen,
          and Graham Kalton, eds. Panel on Estimates of Poverty for Small Geographic
          Areas, Committee on National Statistics, National Research Council. Washington,
          D.C.: National Academy Press.
Ringwelski, M.
   1991   Matching Error—Estimates of Clerical Matching Error from Quality Assurance Re-
          sults. 1990 Coverage Studies and Evaluation Memorandum Series I-2. Bureau of
          the Census, U.S. Department of Commerce, Washington, D.C.
Robinson, J.G., B. Ahmed, P. das Gupta, and K.A. Woodrow
   1993   Estimation of population coverage in the 1990 United States census based on de-
          mographic analysis. *Journal of the American Statistical Association* 88(423):1061-1071.
Schafer, J.L.
   1993   Comment on "Assessing between-block heterogeneity within the post-strata of the
          1990 post-enumeration survey," by Hengartner and Speed. *Journal of the American
          Statistical Association* 88:1125-1127.

Schafer, J.L., M. Khare, and T.M. Ezzati-Rice
  1993 Multiple imputation of missing data in NHANES III. In *Proceedings of the Annual Research Conference, March 21-24, 1993.* Bureau of the Census. Washington, D.C: U.S. Department of Commerce.
Schirm, A.L., and S.H. Preston
  1987 Census undercount adjustment and the quality of geographic population distributions (with discussion). *Journal of the American Statistical Association* 82:965-990.
  1992 Comment on "Should we have adjusted the U.S. census of 1980?" by Freedman and Navidi. *Survey Methodology* 19(1):35-43.
Sekar, C.C., and W.E. Deming
  1949 On a method of estimating birth and death rates and the extent of registration. *Journal of the American Statistical Association* 44:101-115.
Thompson, J. H.
  1992 CAPE Processing Results, Memorandum, March 20, 1992. Bureau of the Census, U.S. Department of Commerce, Washington, D.C.
Tourangeau, R., G. Shapiro, A. Kearney, and L. Ernst
  1997 Who lives here? Survey undercoverage and household roster questions. *Journal of Official Statistics* 13(1):1-18.
Tukey, J.W.
  1983 Affidavit presented to U.S. District Court, Southern District of New York, in *Cuomo v. Baldrige,* 80 Civ. 4550 (JES).
U.S. General Accounting Office
  1992 *Decennial Census. 1990 Results Show Need for Fundamental Reform.* GAO/GGD-92-94. Washington, D.C.: U.S. Government Printing Office.
  1998 *2000 Census. Preparations for Dress Rehearsal Leave Many Unanswered Questions.* GAO/GGD-98-74. Report to the Committee on Governmental Affairs, U.S. Senate. Washington, D.C.: U.S. Government Printing Office.
Waksberg, J.
  1998 The Hansen era: Statistical research and its implementation at the Census Bureau, 1940-1970. *Journal of Official Statistics* 14(2)119-135.
Wolter, K.M.
  1986 Some coverage error models for census data. *Journal of the American Statistical Association* 81 (394):338-346.
Wolter, K.M., and B. Causey
  1991 Evaluation of procedures for improving population estimates for small areas. *Journal of the American Statistical Association* 86:278-284.
Zanutto, E., and A.M. Zaslavsky
  1996 Estimating a Population Roster from an Incomplete Census Using Mailback Questionnaires, Administrative Records, and Sampled Nonresponse Follow-up. Technical report, March 15. Department of Statistics, Harvard University.
Zaslavsky, A.M.
  1988 Representing local area adjustments by reweighting of households. *Survey Methodology* 14:265-288.
  1993 Combining census, dual-system, and evaluation study data to estimate population shares. *Journal of the American Statistical Association* 88:1092-1105.

Biographical Sketches of Panel Members and Staff

KEITH F. RUST (*Chair*) is a vice president and associate director of the statistical group at Westat, Inc. He is also research associate professor at the Joint Program in Survey Methodology, University of Maryland, College Park, and director of statistical operations for the National Assessment of Educational Progress. He was the sampling referee for the Third International Mathematics and Science Study (TIMSS). His primary areas of research are sample survey design, variance estimation, and inference from complex survey data. From 1992 to 1998 he was a member of the Committee on National Statistics, and he is now on the editorial board of the *Journal of Official Statistics*. He received a B.A. from Flinders University of South Australia and an M.S. and a Ph.D. in biostatistics from the University of Michigan.

RONALD F. ABLER is executive director of the Association of American Geographers and a vice president of the International Geographical Union. He serves on the boards of directors of Project Varenius, GIS/LIS, Inc., and the International Geographic Information Foundation and is treasurer of the University Consortium for Geographic Information Sciences. He is professor emeritus of geography at Pennsylvania State University, where he taught from 1967 to 1995, serving as head of the Department of Geography from 1976 to 1982. He was also director of the Geography and Regional Science Program at the National Science Foundation from 1984 to 1988. He was elected a fellow of the American Association for the Advancement of Science in 1985 and was awarded the Centenary Medal of the Royal Scottish Geographical Society in 1990. He received honors from the Association of American Geographers in 1995 and was awarded the Victoria Medal by the Royal Geographical Society's Institute of British Geographers in 1996.

ROBERT M. BELL is a senior statistician and head of the statistics group at Rand. He has worked on many different projects, mainly in health and education. His primary areas of interest are survey design, survey analysis, and general experimental design issues. He received a B.S. in mathematics from Harvey Mudd College, an M.S. in statistics from the University of Chicago, and a Ph.D. in statistics from Stanford University.

GORDON J. BRACKSTONE is assistant chief statistician with responsibility for statistical methodology, computing, and classification systems at Statistics Canada. From 1982 to 1985 he was the director-general of the Methodology Branch of Statistics Canada. Previously, he was responsible for surveys and data acquisition in the Central Statistical Office of British Columbia. His professional work has been in survey methodology, particularly assessment of the quality of census and survey data. He is a fellow of the American Statistical Association and an elected member of the International Statistical Institute. He received B.Sc. and M.Sc. degrees in statistics from the London School of Economics.

MICHAEL L. COHEN, a senior program officer for the Committee on National Statistics, currently works with the Panel on Alternative Census Methodologies and the Panel on Estimates of Poverty for Small Geographic Areas and formerly served as study director of the committee's Panel on Statistical Methods for Testing and Evaluating Defense Systems. Previously, he was a mathematical statistician at the Energy Information Administration, an assistant professor in the School of Public Affairs at the University of Maryland, and a visiting lecturer at the Department of Statistics at Princeton University. His general area of research is the use of statistics in public policy, with particular interest in census undercount, model validation, and robust estimation. He received a B.S. in mathematics from the University of Michigan and an M.S. and a Ph.D. in statistics from Stanford University.

JOHN L. CZAJKA is a senior sociologist at Mathematica Policy Research, Inc. Much of his research has focused on statistical uses of administrative records, analysis of program participation, and the design and analysis of longitudinal data. This work has included designing strategies for handling incomplete data and addressing problems of nonsampling error in a number of contexts. During his many years of research with statistical data developed by the Internal Revenue Service, he prepared a study of the feasibility of using tax records to count the population. More recently he has conducted research on estimating the number of uninsured children at the national and state levels. He received a B.A. in government from Harvard University and a Ph.D. in sociology from the University of Michigan.

MICHEL A. LETTRE is assistant director for planning data services with the Maryland Office of Planning. He has served as the governor's chief staff person on the redistricting advisory committee and also coordinated the governor's 1990 census promotion campaign. His office serves as the principal agency for the distribution of census data in the state of Maryland under the Census Bureau's state data center program. He has an M.S. degree in urban and public affairs from Carnegie Mellon University.

D. BRUCE PETRIE is assistant chief statistician at Statistics Canada, responsible for the agency's programs in the area of social statistics, covering labor, household incomes and expenditures, health, education and culture, demography, and the census. In this capacity he had overall responsibility for the past three Canadian population censuses and is currently supervising preparations for the next census in 2001. He served on a previous National Research Council panel charged with evaluating alternative census methods. He has a bachelor of commerce degree from Dalhousie University and an M.B.A. from the University of Western Ontario.

NATHANIEL SCHENKER is an associate professor in the Department of Biostatistics, School of Public Health, at the University of California, Los Angeles. Previously, he was a mathematical statistician in the Statistical Research Division of the Bureau of the Census. His research interests include missing data, census undercount, survival analysis, and statistical methods for studies of cancer and AIDS. He is a former associate editor of the *Journal of the American Statistical Association*, for which he was also editor of a special section, "Undercount in the 1990 Census." He is a fellow of the American Statistical Association. He received a Ph.D. in statistics from the University of Chicago.

STANLEY K. SMITH is a professor of economics and director of the Bureau of Economic and Business Research, College of Business, at the University of Florida, Gainesville. He is also director of the bureau's population program, which produces the official state and local population estimates and projections for the state of Florida. He is Florida's representative to the federal-state cooperative program for population estimates and projections and a past president of the Southern Demographic Association. His research interests include the methodology and analysis of population estimates and projections and the determinants and consequences of migration. He received a B.A. in history from Goshen College and a Ph.D. in economics from the University of Michigan.

LYNNE STOKES is a professor in the Department of Management Science and Information Systems at the University of Texas at Austin. Her research program is focused in the area of sampling, with an emphasis on assessment of nonsampling errors in surveys. She is a fellow of the American Statistical Association. She received a B.A. from the University of the South and an M.S. and a Ph.D. from the University of North Carolina at Chapel Hill.

JAMES TRUSSELL is professor of economics and public affairs, faculty associate of the Office of Population Research, and associate dean of the Woodrow Wilson School of Public and International Affairs at Princeton University. He is the author or coauthor of more than 150 scientific publications, primarily in the areas of reproductive health and demographic methodology. He has served on many National Research Council panels, including two previous ones on the census. He received a B.S. in mathematics from Davidson College, a B.Phil. in economics from Oxford University, and a Ph.D. in economics from Princeton University.

ANDREW A. WHITE is deputy director of the Committee on National Statistics and has served or is currently serving as study director for the Panel on Alternative Census Methodologies, the Panel to Review the Statistical Procedures of the Decennial Census, and the Panel to Study the Research Program of the Economic Research Service. He is a former survey designer, research staff chief, and executive staff member of the National Center for Health Statistics and was a consulting statistician with the Michigan Department of Public Health. He directed interdisciplinary research in statistical mapping, survey design, and work in customer satisfaction. He received a B.A. in political science and an M.P.H. and a Ph.D. in biostatistics from the University of Michigan.

ALAN M. ZASLAVSKY is associate professor of statistics in the Department of Health Care Policy at Harvard Medical School. He was formerly on the faculty of the Department of Statistics at Harvard. His research interests include measurement of quality in health care, census methodology, estimation and correction of census undercount, small-area estimation, microsimulation, design and analysis of surveys, and Bayesian methods. In addition to this panel, he has served or is serving on other panels of the Committee on National Statistics concerned with census methods and with evaluation of small-area estimates of poverty. He is a fellow of the American Statistical Association. He received a Ph.D. in applied mathematics from the Massachusetts Institute of Technology.